COMPASS AND MAP NAVIGATOR

THE COMPLETE GUIDE TO STAYING FOUND

BY MICHAEL HODGSON

ICS BOOKS, Inc.

Merrillville, IN

Published by:
The Brunton Company
620 East Monroe
Riverton, WY 82501
307-856-6559

Co-Published by:
ICS Books, Inc.
1370 E. 86th Place
Merrillville, IN 46410
800-541-7323

Library of Congress Cataloging-in-Publication Data

Hodgson, Michael.
    The compass and map navigator : The Complete Guide to Staying Found / by Michael Hodgson.
        p. cm.
    Includes index.
    ISBN 1–57034–043–9
    1. Map reading. 2. Navigation. I. Title.
GA151.H57   1996
796.5′ 1—dc20

96–9934
CIP

To Johnny "the-man-the-myth-the-legend" Dodd,
Beth Howard, Dan Glick, and Roy Wallack—my
Eco-Challenge teammates, who helped to guide
my soul while I guided their steps.

Contents

Introduction

- **Anyone Can Stay on the Right Path,
  Given the Right Tools**

ANYONE CAN STAY ON THE RIGHT PATH, GIVEN THE RIGHT TOOLS

Which way!? Our team of journalists competing in the first Eco-Challenge (a 360-mile, nonstop adventure race by foot, paddle, mountain bike, and climbing rope) stood on top of a ridge, gazing across a jumbled landscape of rocks and canyons. The faint tracks before us could be trails or just tracks from others who had gotten lost. Other teams milled about in a confused fashion. We had all hiked 70 miles across some very unforgiving desert terrain in just under a day-and-a-half. Many of us were almost out of water. A few of the teams had members who appeared to be on the verge of collapse.

I tried to block out the distractions and focus on the task at hand—getting us on the right path and to the next water hole before we all ran dry. As the team navigator, the pressure rested squarely on my shoulders. The sun began to set, washing out essential features and details on the landscape. I had to work quickly.

Taking mental pictures of the landscape, I tucked shapes away into my mind for future reference. Then, I shot several key bearings with my compass and plotted a course. The path that became clear to me headed in a direction that appeared to make no logical sense—unless you factored in all the bits of information available. I headed off resolutely, although there was no denying the tiny lump in my throat . . . What if I were wrong? Every few hundred feet I glanced around, taking more mental pictures, comparing them with what I knew the map said, and placing us on the map accordingly.

A blanket of darkness wrapped around us, leaving me no choice but to work with silhouettes, my map and compass, and the stars above. One of my teammates, Johnny Dodd, told me to glance back up the trail. There, strung out behind me, were more than twenty-five bobbing headlamps, representing five other teams. I had become the Pied Piper, hopefully leading them to life-sustaining water.

We came to a fork in the road and a debate ensued. Most of the footprints from teams before headed right. My instincts and navigational information indicated that left was the correct choice. My team backed my choice so off we headed, with the other teams right behind. The night became an epic, with us arriving at the watering hole (I was correct) at 4:00 a.m. A number of other teams got hopelessly lost going through the same terrain—probably because they didn't have all the requisite skills or experience needed to see them through the navigational challenges. I managed to get us where we needed to be only because I studied every piece of the navigation puzzle before me and then fit each piece together until it made sense.

Why do people get lost? There are many reasons, and most of them are completely avoidable. The most common mistake is not packing a map and compass because you're "just going out for a quick hike on a clearly marked trail." All you have to do is be daydreaming or chatting with your partners, and you may walk off one trail and onto another, completely unaware. Another mistake is lack of preparation. Instead, the trip is on, so you grab a map, toss the compass in the pack, and go, with no forethought or proper map homework. I always study my maps before I go out, which is why I probably have an easier time staying on course. Yet another reason is blindly trusting your partner, who may be just as hopelessly lost as you. Everyone who wants to safely enjoy the great outdoors should master basic navigational skills and be able to use them.

Having been a member of several search and rescue teams and also a professional mountain guide, I am continually amazed by the number of people I encounter who dutifully carry along a map and shiny new compass, yet have absolutely no idea where they are, where they are heading, or where they came from. Sure, packing along a topographic map and a compass fulfill two of the "ten essentials" for safe backcountry travel, but what good are they if you don't know how to use them? Not much! You may as well pack a world atlas or road map because without map and compass skills, a road map will be as good as a regular topographic map in the backcountry.

There is an art to staying found that involves using one's head, remaining observant, and applying map and compass skills properly. The basic skills involved in simple navigation are not all that hard to acquire. What follows is a very easy-to-use guide to staying found. It includes illustrations and diagrams, courtesy of the folks at Brunton, to assist you in picking the right tools, learning how to use them and help you stay on course.

With this book and a bit of practice, you'll soon be able to say with confidence that you, like the author (a.k.a. "navgod" to his friends and fellow adventure racing competitors), have never been lost— disoriented for a few days maybe, but never lost.

Happy Trails!

Chapter One

The Foundation of Navigation

- The History of Navigation
- Maintaining Your Sense of Direction . . . Naturally
- On Staying Found When You Suspect You're Lost

THE HISTORY OF NAVIGATION

Before the invention of the compass, early travelers and mariners navigated by the lay of the land as well as the position of the sun and stars. The Vikings, possibly some of the greatest and most skilled adventurers of their time, relied completely on the position of the sun and stars to find their way across the ocean and back home again. Whenever these celestial bodies were obscured by fog or clouds, the Vikings simply drifted until the weather cleared.

Early Sumarians, Cretans, Egyptians, Phoenicians, Greeks, Romans, and Scandinavians navigated on the sea by hugging a coastline and identifying their position in relation to known objects on land. These mariners traveled by day and rested at night. None of them had maps or charts, although some relied on a list of directions that identified landmarks, anchorages, and hazards such as shoals and reefs.

Land explorers had both maps and lists. However, since few ventured far from home, the maps were useful only to armies and traders. The oldest known surviving maps come from Mesopotamia and are etched into clay tablets. Although there are references to older maps in Greek and Roman writings, these maps were drawn onto parchment paper and have since disappeared.

During the twelfth century, the first crude compass was created. It resulted from the discovery that the magnetized iron found in lodestone would align itself in a north/south fashion if floated on a piece of wood in a container of water. Shortly thereafter, it was discovered that magnetizing an iron or steel needle would cause the needle to align itself also in a north/south fashion.

This compass was used first by the Chinese and by early explorers in European countries. The ability of the early compass designs, as well as today's modern versions, to function is due to the physical properties of the earth; it's really just a huge magnet. The earth's poles (or points of polarity) are oval areas located approximately thirteen hundred miles from geographic North and South Poles. A magnetized needle simply aligns itself with the irregular lines of magnetic force that connect the north and south points. In a few places on Earth, the magnetic lines of force happen to match the meridians of geographic North and South. In most cases, however, the magnetic needle points a few degrees to the east or west of geographic (true) North. This is known as "declination," which I will explain in detail later.

Despite the development of the compass, it wasn't until the late seventeenth century, when astronomical discoveries linked with mapmaking techniques allowed for the designation of lines of longitude, that maps began to come of age and navigation leapt forward. For the first time, the location of specific places was accurately determined and mapped. This led to an increased accuracy of mapping coastlines in eighteenth century maps.

During the nineteenth century, land exploration began to explode as armies and teams of adventurers took off in earnest to claim places unknown (to them at least) for king, queen, country, and their own glory. This exploration of continental interiors began to fill the voids in the maps. The scientific community was a driving force in the push to map distant lands; numerous scholarly and scientific studies of the Earth were undertaken.

The real father of today's modern compass was David W. Brunton. Brunton invented a device known as the Pocket Transit, a professional surveyor's instrument, in 1894 (Figure 1–1). Still, the principals of this instrument were the same as those used by the Chinese (who floated a magnetized needle on a straw or splinter of wood in a bowl of water) or the Arab mariners (who, it is reported, suspended a magnetized piece of iron from a piece of string). And, believe it or not, the compasses you use today, although made of far more modern materials, rely on the same principals—a magnetized piece of metal is allowed to rotate freely in solution as it seeks magnetic north.

Figure 1–1 Brunton Pocket Transit surveying compass. Developed by David Brunton, a mining engineer, and patented in 1894.

Through the use of surveying tools and international cooperation, the twentieth century has seen dramatic improvement in mapping coverage. Cooperative efforts, such as the joint venture between the United States and a number of Latin American governments, dubbed the Inter-American Geodetic Survey, resulted in the production of fairly accurate maps for much of the Western Hemisphere by 1970.

Still, not all of the world has been mapped, and some of what has been mapped has not been mapped very well. I was trekking in Baja a number of years back and became very confused by what the land and my eyes were telling me and what the Mexican-produced topographic map said I should be seeing. After much consternation and scouting, I came to realize that the mountain I was standing on was the one the map said was ten miles distant, and the mountain I was looking at was, in fact, the mountain the map said I was standing on. A MAJOR ten-mile flip-flop error by both a surveyor and a cartographer. Lesson: Never trust what a map has to say unless you can prove it through careful observation and compass use.

MAINTAINING YOUR SENSE OF DIRECTION . . . NATURALLY

While no one can honestly claim to have an infallible sense of direction, the key to staying found and knowing where you are most of the time is simply this: Stay alert to your surroundings. The best navigators stay on course by using their eyes, their ears, their nose, and their wit (as well as their knowledge of map and compass skills)—all in relationship with each other. My daughter Nicole often jokes that while I never seem to get lost when I'm outdoors, inside a mall I'm absolutely hopeless, and she's basically right. In a mall, I tend to tune out and consequently remove myself from the changing pictures as I walk, setting myself up time and again to wonder Where in the @#$% is the main entrance and where did I leave the car? If I would just take a lesson from my own words, "Stay alert," I might not have such urban challenges.

Accurate navigation begins with 360-degree awareness 100 percent of the time. The eyes should always be searching, seeking clues to the course you are on. Pay close attention to trees, logs, rocks, hills, ridges, streams, and even man-made landmarks as you pass them. Make mental notes as you go. Look over your shoulder so that you can view how the features may change as you move along. When I taught advanced map and compass courses, most students would work on cruise control finding their way from point A to point B. Yet, invariably, they would question themselves and the route if asked to try to head back the way they came and return to point A. Why? Because what may seem intimately familiar going one way takes on an entirely different face from the other side. Get in the habit of looking forward, from side-to-side, and over your shoulder as you walk along (Figure 1–2).

Take note of your directional changes and associate them with the terrain surrounding you. Keep putting together, rather like assembling a puzzle, all the different features of the various landmarks you are passing. Continually ask yourself, "If I had to return to where I started right now, how would I go?" Although you may not be using a compass, try to think directionally. The hill you are going around right now lies to the east while that tall pine standing out in the middle of the meadow ahead marks north. Keep track of all trail intersections, stream crossings, major elevation changes, and other significant

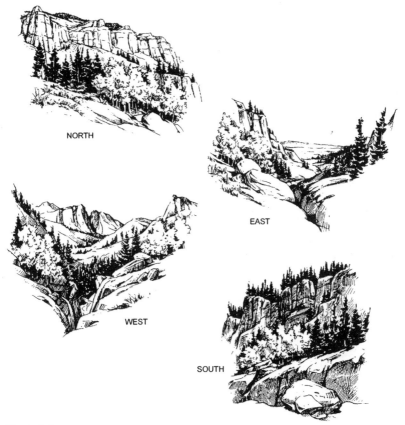

Figure 1–2

features. Each piece you observe becomes a critical part of the entire picture you must assemble in order for you, and perhaps your group, to stay the course.

Don't forget to take into account the sky as well. Although the sun moves across the sky (as does the moon) as the earth spins, learning to associate times of day with the sun's position in relation to landmarks you are passing can be immensely helpful in determining where you are should you need to retrace your steps. Using the sun and a watch or even a stick in the ground to determine direction also is useful as I will demonstrate later in this book.

Navigation relies strongly on your ears and nose, too. You may not be able to see the stream, but if you can hear it, make a note where it lies and estimate how far away it is. If you drop into a valley and it feels far cooler than other valleys you have passed through that day, make a note. Perhaps you are walking through a grove of trees or across a meadow and notice a unique odor—the pungent aroma of wild onion or the scent of cedar—make a mental note.

Using eyes, ears, and nose to stay on course is the way pioneers and Native Americans used to navigate successfully across terrain much wilder than it is now—all without the aid of a compass or map. You can do it, too, with a lot of practice.

ON STAYING FOUND WHEN YOU SUSPECT YOU'RE LOST

It has been rumored that famed outdoorsman Daniel Boone was never lost, although he did admit to being "mighty disoriented for a week or two." In this day and age of search and rescue teams, maps, compasses, and high technology, lost most often means that you will be late for dinner. At worst, it generally means that someone else will find you. The following are some tips aimed at helping you and your loved ones stay found:

- Always tell a family member or close friend where you are going, when you will be leaving, and when you plan on returning—and then stick to your plan.

- Be prepared for the worst. Just because you are heading out for a day hike under sunny skies doesn't mean you won't be forced to spend a night out under adverse weather conditions. Extra food and clothing are a minimum must. Carry a lightweight survival kit with a space blanket, a plastic tarp, nylon cord, waterproof matches, a fire starter, a whistle, a signal mirror, water purification tablets, a metal cup in which to heat water, a small flashlight, and a knife.

- Don't just carry a map and compass; become proficient at using these tools. This book is an excellent place to begin your proficiency training, but reading alone will not do you much good. You must get out and practice, practice, practice. Joining an orienteering club near you is a great way to gain experience and to have a lot of fun.

- Pay attention to your surroundings. Staying on the correct path and then being able to find your way back again requires 360-

degree observation. Make mental notes of landmarks as you are walking toward them and then as you are walking away from them.

- Should you get lost, don't panic. Recognize the difficulty, and then rationally work your way through it. Most often, if you sit down and calmly reflect for a few minutes, mentally retracing your steps, the solution to the situation becomes clear.

- If you come to the conclusion you are definitely lost, STAY PUT! Although it is tempting to wander, there are numerous tales of lost individuals being found dead weeks or months after a search was begun, simply because they wandered out of the area where the search and rescue crew expected them to be.

- Drink plenty of water. Your body can do without food for a few days, but it cannot function without water. Signal your position by building a smoky fire. If you run out of food, don't eat anything unless you are sure you can identify it as edible.

- Shelter yourself from the elements as best you can. Use the tarp in your survival kit to fashion a lean-to. Use dry leaves and other dry plant debris (not poison oak or stinging nettles) to insulate you from the cold ground.

Chapter Two

Understanding the Language of Maps

- **What Is a Topographic Map?**
- **To Understand a Map, You Must First Understand What Information May Be Found Around Its Border or Margin**
- **Reading the Lay of the Land from the Story Your Map Tells**
- **Using Your Map's Scale to Estimate Trip Distance**
- **Creating a Trail Profile**
- **Finding Yourself on the Map**
- **Orienting a Map without a Compass**
- **Caring for Your Map**
- **Folding a Map**
- **A Map Has Its Limitations**

WHAT IS A TOPOGRAPHIC MAP?

A topographic map represents the three-dimensional lay of the land. It does this by using contour lines to show where hills, mountains, valleys, and canyons are located. A trained eye will see the three-dimensional images. Topographic maps are printed in color with green depicting forested or vegetated areas and white indicating open terrain. Contour or elevation lines are printed in brown. Blue indicates water—either a lake, river or stream. Black is used for man-made features such as trails, roads, and buildings. Man-made features on topographic maps other than privately produced ones such as those printed by Trails Illustrated, DeLorme, Earthwalk, and Harrison should be suspect; many USGS (United States Geological Survey) maps have not been revised in over twenty years. There are many other symbols used to depict such things as mines, ghost towns, marshes, swamps, waterfalls, and caves. The USGS does not print a key on each of its topographic maps, but rather on a separate sheet that may be obtained free from the USGS.

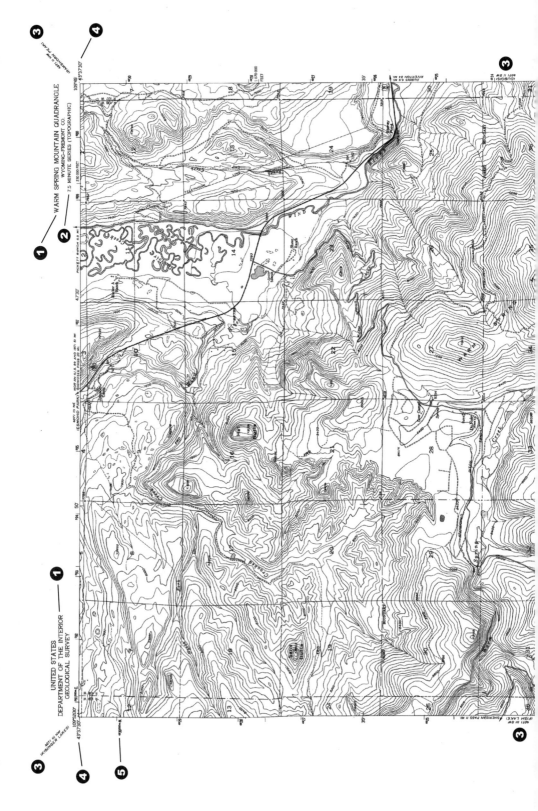

Figure 2–1

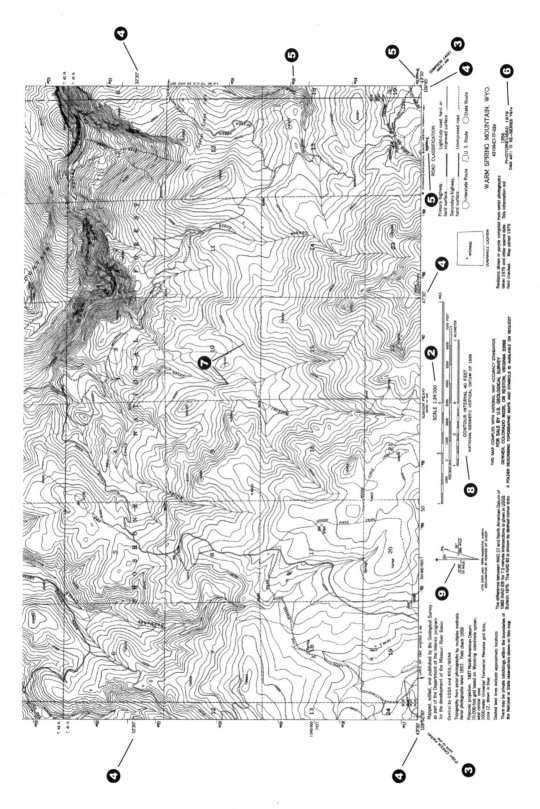

See Appendix A–4 for topographical maps printed since 1992.

TO UNDERSTAND A MAP, YOU MUST FIRST UNDERSTAND WHAT INFORMATION MAY BE FOUND AROUND ITS BORDER OR MARGIN

Around the edge of any map, you will find numerous symbols, dashes, crosshatches, numbers, and words that offer essential meaning to the information printed on the map itself. The following list of numbered items correspond with the sample USGS topographic map on pages 20–21 (Figure 2–1).

❶ Who's map is it and what area does it represent?

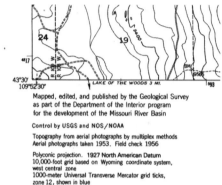

Mapped, edited, and published by the Geological Survey as part of the Department of the Interior program for the development of the Missouri River Basin

Control by USGS and NOS/NOAA

Topography from aerial photographs by multiplex methods
Aerial photographs taken 1953. Field check 1956

Polyconic projection. 1927 North American Datum
10,000-foot grid based on Wyoming coordinate system,
west central zone
1000-meter Universal Transverse Mercator grid ticks,
zone 12, shown in blue

Dashed land lines indicate approximate locations

There may be private inholdings within the boundaries of
the National or State reservations shown on this map

Figure 2–2

Somewhere on the map will be information regarding the map's creator or publisher and also the area the map covers. With USGS maps, the publishing information appears in the lower left corner along the white border surrounding the map itself (Figure 2–2). The area the map covers will be indicated in the upper right corner along the white border on a USGS map (Figure 2–3). The United States is divided into quadrants based on lines of latitude and longitude, and each quadrant most often carries the name of a significant geographical feature or municipality falling within the quadrant's boundaries.

❷ What is the map's size (area of coverage) and scale?

USGS prints its maps in what are known as series (e.g. the 7.5 minute series, the 15 minute series). Although you can still find 15 minute series maps, the USGS prints primarily 7.5 minute series maps these days. To explain minutes, the earth is divided into 360 degrees of latitude (designating east and west) and 180 degrees of longitude (designating north and south). Each degree is divided into sixty units of measurement called

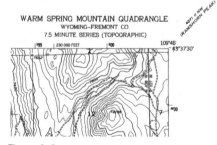

Figure 2–3

Figure 2–4

"minutes," and each minute is divided into sixty units of measurement called "seconds." In navigational terms, minutes and seconds have absolutely nothing to do with time and everything to do with distance. A 7.5 minute series map represents an area of the earth's surface that is 7.5 minutes (one-eighth of a degree) of longitude wide by 7.5 minutes (one-eighth of a degree) of latitude high (Figure 2–4).

Typically, in a 7.5 minute map, the scale will be 1:24,000, which means that every one unit of measurement on the map will equal 24,000 units of the same measurement full-sized. In a 1:24,000 scale map, one inch equals about four-tenths of a mile or nearly 2,000 feet. A 15 minute map is typically 1:62,500 which translates roughly to one inch equaling one mile. For navigational purposes, you will also find maps that are scaled 1:250,000 or one inch equaling four miles. This larger scale of map is useful for planning your trip since it affords a big-picture, birds-eye view of the terrain you will be crossing. However, the map's scale is really too big to offer useful information when detailed map-in-the-hand field navigation is required (see Appendix Figure A–3).

At the bottom of most maps will be a bar scale that will allow you to measure distances that correspond to feet, miles, and/or kilometer (Figure 2–5).

❸ What maps adjoin the one you are looking at?

Most maps will print adjoining map information along their borders so that you can effectively link maps of the same series/scale and publisher. Typically, the names of corresponding and adjoining maps may be found printed at each corner, at each side, and at both the top and bottom of the map (Figure 2–6). Many maps will also print a silhouette picture of the region the map

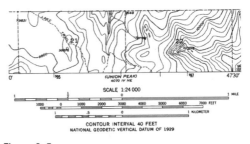

Figure 2–5

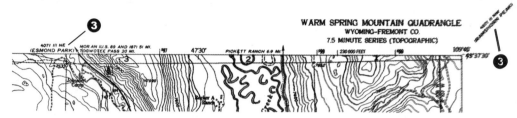

Figure 2–6

series covers, divided into equal quadrants; the map you are using will be the one that is shaded. This way you can visually see where the map fits into the entire region's mapping picture and how many adjoining maps might be required to navigate across it.

❹ Find latitude and longitude.

Degrees of latitude and longitude are indicated in the corners of most maps. Reading up from the bottom left or right corner of a map, changes in minutes and seconds of latitude (degrees are usually omitted unless the scale is so large that these too change between corners) are indicated by black ticks and/or fine black lines. Latitude in the Northern Hemisphere (north of the equator) increases as you move north and toward the top of the map. Reading left from the bottom right or top right corner of a map, changes in minutes and seconds of longitude (degrees are usually omitted unless the scale is so large that these too change between corners) are indicated by black ticks and/or fine black lines. Longitude in the Western Hemisphere (west of the International Date Line running through Greenwich, England) increases as you go west up to 180 degrees. At 180 degrees, you enter the Eastern Hemisphere and longitude will begin to decrease (Figure 2–7).

On each map, a pattern of squares or rectangles—called coordinate grids—will be printed. These grids are made up of intersecting latitude and longitude lines and/or intersecting UTM easting and northing lines (UTM or Universal Transverse Mercator is explained below). Each location on a map corresponds to a unique set of coordinates that can be described by the corresponding latitude and longitude lines. Finding that location then becomes easy by simply connecting the indicated lines of latitude and longitude (or the UTM

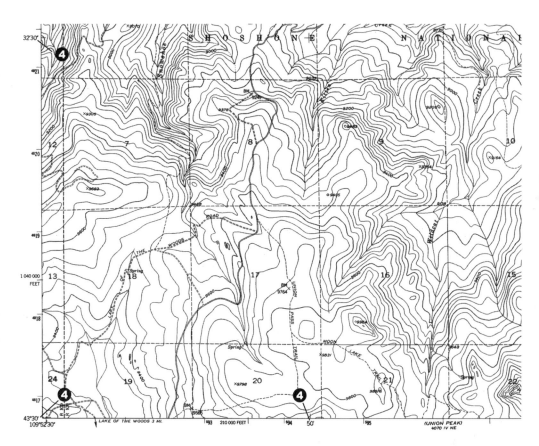

Figure 2–7

easting and northing lines) found marked along the map's borders (Figure 2–8).

❺ Universal Transverse Mercator (UTM)—Say what?

UTM refers to the system grid that divides the entire world into sixty zones that are 6 degrees wide. The zones begin at east/west longitude 180 degrees and continue at 6-degree intervals. Each zone is then removed from the globe and flattened, losing its relationship to a sphere and introducing a certain amount of distortion. Since UTM projections distort the regions above 84 degrees north latitude and below 80 degrees south latitude far too much, they are not covered by maps using the UTM grid. The UTM grid is based upon the meter, and

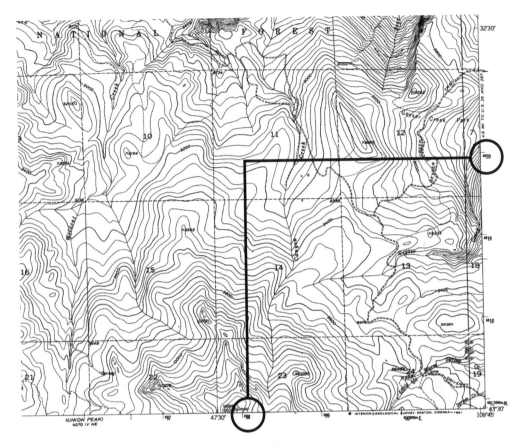

Figure 2–8

grid lines are always one kilometer (.62 miles) apart, making it much easier to estimate distance on a map. UTM coordinates are printed on a map to indicate east/west and north/south positions (Figure 2–9). Numbers along the right side of a map are called northings (indicating the exact position north or south). Numbers along the top of the map are called eastings (indicating the exact position east or west).

Making sense of the numbers is quick and easy:

- Increasing easting numbers indicate you are heading east; decreasing numbers indicate you are heading west. Increasing northing numbers indicate you are heading north; decreasing numbers indicate you are heading south.

- A reading of full UTM positions written along the right side of your map might go as follows: first mark (⁴35⁰⁰⁰m.N.) and then the second mark (⁴36⁰⁰⁰m.N.). What does this mean? The larger numbers (35 and 36) indicate thousands of meters, and since a thousand meters equals one kilometer, the two ticks are one thousand meters or one kilometer apart. The last three numbers are printed smaller and indicate hundreds of meters. If the readings of the marks were (⁴35⁰⁰⁰m.N.) and then (⁴35⁵⁰⁰m.N.), this would indicate the ticks were five hundred meters or one-half a kilometer apart.

You will need to understand UTM if you plan on working with a GPS (global positioning system) or if you plan on using maps other than those printed by the USGS. The Bureau of Land Management (BLM) relies on the UTM system heavily. Many guidebooks and

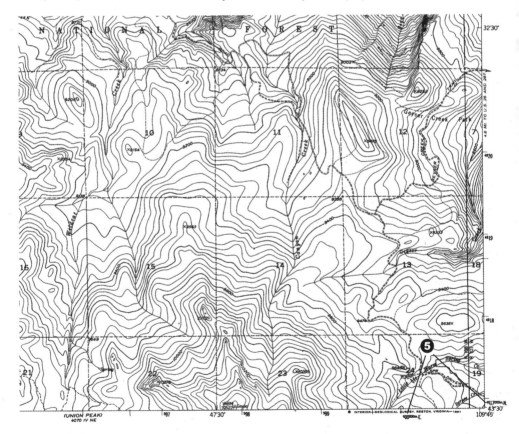

Figure 2–9

directions offered in descriptions give UTM bearings rather than latitude and longitude coordinates.

❻ Revisions.

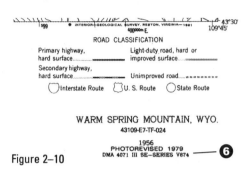

Figure 2–10

ROAD CLASSIFICATION

Primary highway, hard surface............................. Light-duty road, hard or improved surface...............

Secondary highway, hard surface............................. Unimproved road............

◯ Interstate Route   ◯ U. S. Route   ◯ State Route

WARM SPRING MOUNTAIN, WYO.
43109-E7-TF-024
1956
PHOTOREVISED 1979
DMA 4071 III SE—SERIES V874 ——— **❻**

Updates to USGS topographical maps will be printed in the color purple with the date of the update appearing directly below the original map printing date in the lower right corner (Figure 2–10; see also Appendix Figure A–4). These updates are only photo revised changes and do not reflect actual field checking. This is very useful information on USGS topographical maps since the original surveys and data on which a map is based are often very old (no sense wasting valuable time and energy trying to find a trail that hasn't existed in decades even though it appears on this fifty-year-old map).

❼ Contour lines.

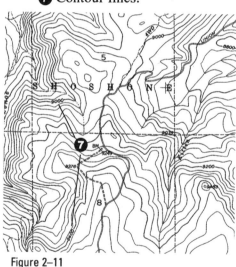

Figure 2–11

Contour lines are the brown squiggly lines on a topographic map that appear rather confusing at first glance, but are really precise representations of geography in the area the map represents. Each contour line comprises an often irregular closed loop that connects points of equal elevation. The line with a darker shade of brown, typically every fifth line, is called an index contour and usually has the elevation printed on it (Figure 2–11).

❽ Contour interval.

To correctly read the severity of the terrain's ups and downs, you must determine the contour interval, printed at the bottom of the map.

The contour interval indicates the elevation change
between adjacent contour
lines (Figure 2–12).

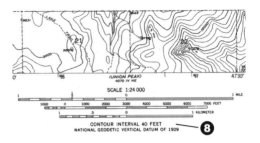

Figure 2–12

9 Declination.

At the bottom of each
map will be a declination
illustration. The diagram will
show three variations in direction: The geographic North Pole,
indicated by a line with star on the top of it and pointing toward the top
of the globe; the magnetic north pole, indicated by a line with MN on the
top of it and pointing toward the magnetic north pole (the area a magnetic
needle on a compass points to); and the grid north pole, a line with GN
on the top of it. Grid north pole refers to the Universal Transverse
Mercator Grid designed by cartographers to reduce the distortion created
by transferring the earth's curvature to a flat map surface. For the
purposes of declination, only geographic North and magnetic north and
the degree of difference east or west between the two are of importance
here. The degrees of declination will be printed alongside the illustration.
You can determine if the indicated declination is east or west depending
on which side of the geographic North Pole line the magnetic north pole
line is printed. If it is printed to the right, it is an east declination; to the
left, a west declination. This is important because it will indicate whether
or not you add or subtract degrees to correct your compass reading
(Figure 2–13; see also Appendix A–4).

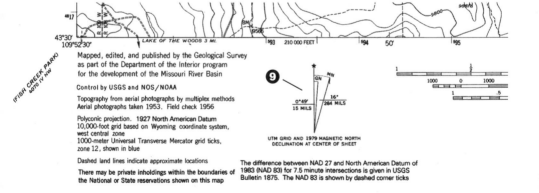

Figure 2–13

READING THE LAY OF THE LAND
FROM THE STORY YOUR MAP TELLS

How do you read contour lines?

In general:

- Widely spaced contour lines indicate a gradual slope.
- The more packed the contour lines are together, the steeper and more severe the terrain. Closely spaced contours may mean a cliff.
- Contours that roughly form circles, each getting smaller in size with each gain in elevation indicate hills or mountain peaks. A summit is often marked with an X and a number printed next to it indicating the exact elevation of that peak (Figure 2–14).

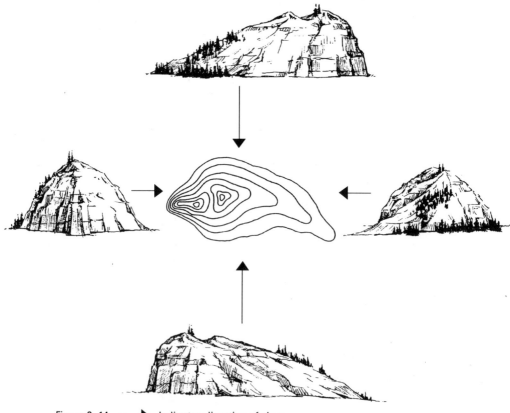

Figure 2–14 ⟶ Indicates direction of view.

- Contour lines that bend into a V shapes (the Vs may look more like Us if the terrain is sloping very gently) represent either a canyon or a sloping ridge. If the V is pointing uphill, toward a point of higher elevation then the Vs are forming a canyon. If the V is pointing downhill, toward a point of lower elevation, then the Vs form a ridge. It stands to reason that a stream in a V would indicate that the V is a canyon pointing towards higher elevations.

- V-shaped valleys on a map are typically steep in nature and more difficult to navigate. On extremely pronounced V shapes, expect the side walls of the canyon to be steep and almost impossible to scramble up or down. Once on the canyon floor, you're probably there to stay until you exit either upstream or downstream. U-shaped valleys, on the other hand, are far

Figure 2–15

more gentle and, consequently, easier to navigate through (Figure 2–15).

How significant is the map's contour interval?

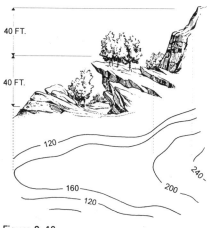

40 FT.

40 FT.

120

160

120

200

240

Figure 2–16

Aside from telling you how steep the terrain is, the interval will offer another bit of critical information. Consider a map with a contour interval of forty feet. This means the cartographer drew a contour line on the map for every forty feet of elevation change up or down. What this also means is that the rather large (to you when standing in front of it) thirty-foot rocky outcropping, or thirty-five–foot cliff, or twenty-five–foot deep wash, won't show up on the map if it falls between the appointed contour interval markings (Figure 2–16).

Just because the map doesn't show a geographic feature does not mean that the feature doesn't exist. I have seen countless navigational errors—I've even made a few myself—because of a geographic feature that isn't on the map. This mystical feature, when viewed within the context of "this map tells the entire truth so that feature must be this feature on the map (even though it isn't)" and "it must be right here which means we are right there (even though you aren't)," can really ruin your day—OOPS! Keep in mind that if you are standing directly in front of the thirty-five–foot rocky hill that isn't on the map, it will also be blocking from your view features that do exist on the map, making orienting that much more difficult unless you are able to determine the interference and move to a better vantage point.

Your use of any map and its ability to be able to help you find your way are only as good as your ability to interpret the size and shape of the geography and relate it to the map that's interpreting it. You must also remember that the map is only one part of the navigational puzzle and you need all the pieces in order to find your way with consistent accuracy.

USING YOUR MAP'S SCALE TO ESTIMATE TRIP DISTANCE

Estimating the distance of your trip is useful if you wish to ensure that you can actually complete the trip in a safe period of time. Of course, distance is only one part of the equation. You must also factor in elevation loss and gain, which will make your route longer and increase the effort required to travel it, adding in effect to the time needed to get from point A to B.

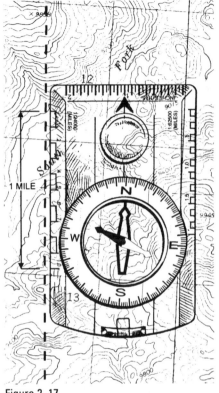

Figure 2–17

Although the bar scale printed at the bottom of your map is straight, I have yet to find many naturally occurring straight lines in the great outdoors. Trails, waterways, and canyons meander from here to there, making it that much more difficult, though not impossible, to estimate how far, how long.

There are a number of measuring wheels on the market, some of which actually work quite well. Still, they aren't perfect; they are added bulk to carry into the field and they must be used very carefully on an absolutely flat surface. Many compasses also include map measuring scales on their baseplates, but again, these require a certain amount of calculation and offer only very rough "straight point-A-to-point-B" measuring (Figure 2–17). My preferred method of measuring distance relies on narrow gauge electrical wire, colored white or red. Electrical wire—the kind used in model building—is very flexible, holds its shape, doesn't stretch, and can be marked with an indelible ink marker. Cut a twelve-inch section of the wire and then mark

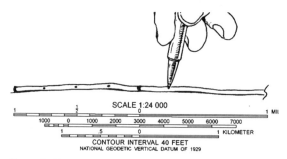

Figure 2–18

quarter-mile and one-mile increments on it with a fine-tipped indelible black ink marker. I have found that using dots for the quarter-mile marks and a complete band around the wire for the one-mile marks works best. Be sure to meticulously match your marks to those on the map's bar scale (Figure 2–18).

Place one end of the wire at your starting point and then gradually bend and contour the wire to match the twists and bends of your trail or route of travel (Figure 2–19). Once the bending and contouring is

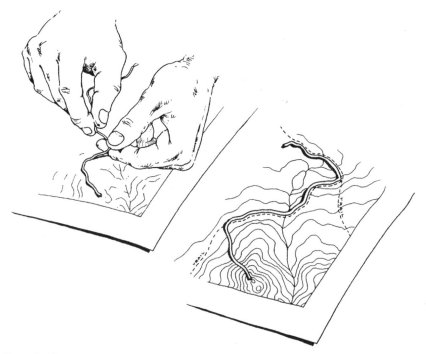

Figure 2–19

finished, you can count up the miles and determine just how far your planned route is, how far it might be to your estimated rest points, and how far it is to points of scenic interest, water, and other landmarks. With the wire in place, you can also assemble a fairly decent trail profile which will afford a very reality-based image of how steep the ups and downs really are.

CREATING A TRAIL PROFILE

One mile as the crow flies is not necessarily representative of one mile as the trail climbs. For one thing, although the horizontal distance may reflect one mile of distance, the hypotenuse (oh gawd . . . it's math. Hypotenuse: the side of a right-angled triangle that is opposite the right angle) is longer if the vertical distance or elevation gained is greater. Huh?! OK, check out the diagram (Figure 2-20). It's also quite difficult to estimate just how steep the route you are going to travel might be. This is where a good trail profile comes in.

Now on my computer generated maps, all I do is press a button and, presto, a neat trail profile appears on the screen. In most instances though, the area I am traveling is not covered by a computerized map. Soooo, I must resort to manual modes of estimation, which is why we left the wire in place after estimating our travel distance. Grab a sheet of paper and draw a straight vertical line up the left side. Beginning at

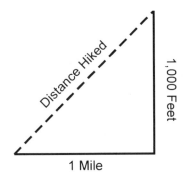

Figure 2–20 Actual Distance hiked is more then one mile.

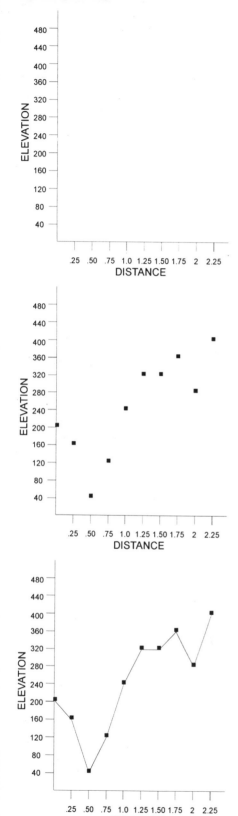

the bottom of the vertical line, draw a horizontal line at a 90-degree angle and across the page to the right. Place marks on the vertical line that represent the contour interval found on the map, working upward from the point of lowest elevation on your route of travel to the highest. Along the horizontal line, place marks every quarter-mile, matching the bar scale on the map. Using a pencil, draw horizontal lines for every contour line, and draw vertical lines for every half-mile interval (every quarter-mile gets to be a bit much and it is easy enough to estimate the middle of a short line to mark quarter-mile increments if needed).

With pencil in hand, begin visually traveling along the wire following your route of travel, first marking the point of elevation at mile zero and then points of elevation for every quarter mile of distance traveled. Once you have all the points marked on your paper graph, connect the dots and, presto, you'll have a very enlightening visual presentation that should demonstrate just what you are in for (Figure 2–21).

FINDING YOURSELF ON THE MAP

A map is of absolutely no use to you unless you can place yourself somewhere on it with accuracy and then be

Figure 2–21

able to determine where you might want to head or where you have come from. To do this, you must first orient the map so that it represents a one-dimensional image that comes as close as possible to paralleling the three-dimensional world you are standing in; the map and

Figure 2–22

the real world become one in your mind (Figure 2–22).

ORIENTING A MAP WITHOUT A COMPASS

The easiest way to orient a map is by using readily identifiable landmarks. This is easier said than done, however, if you have no idea where you are right now. First, you have to determine roughly where you are on the map. Again, landmarks offer the best clues. If you can easily and assuredly identify a nearby landmark (e.g., a readily identifiable peak, a well-known and easily recognized river, a fire tower, a major roadway or trail, or a sign) that is unique enough to have a map symbol or designation, then you are home free. Of course, there is the possibility that while you may be able to recognize a road, trail, river, or shoreline, you may not be able to tell where you are on it. No matter. Roads, trails, fencelines, powerlines, rivers, shorelines and similar landmarks fall under the wonderful category of a "baseline." A baseline is an easily identified feature of length that stands out and is clearly marked on the map. Once you find yourself on a baseline, you simply walk up and down it until you come to another identifiable point. It could even be another baseline intersecting the one you are on. You can now place yourself most assuredly on the map. If you think about it, whenever you offer up directions, you probably give intersecting baselines as a means of helping others. "My house is right near the intersection of Mountain

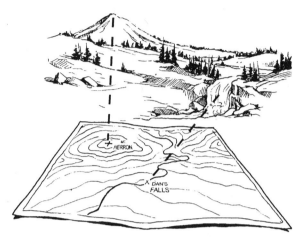

Figure 2–23

Avenue (one baseline) and River Boulevard (another baseline) (Figure 2–23)."

Once you know your exact position on the map, it becomes a fairly simple matter to spin the map until other points of reference on the map line up with the same points of reference found before you on the surrounding landscape. Good navigators will keep their maps in constant orientation to the surrounding landscape as they travel. Yes, this means that sometimes the maps are upside down, which makes it a bit creative when reading map symbols and names, but this is far better than carrying the map right way up and trying mentally to rotate the landscape or the map to compensate. The latter method is pure idiocy in my opinion. Learning to read upside down is far easier and has less potential for navigational disaster.

What if you can orient the map successfully, but still don't know exactly where you are?

Sometimes the surrounding landscape is so big or unique that it is an easy task to orient the map. This is often the case in a desert environment when distant landmarks are readily visible and identifiable, making map orientation a relatively simple process. But how do you know just where you are in the vast expanse of unrecognizable bumps and sandy or rocky undulations? Easy. Pick out three identifiable landmarks, preferably one ahead to the right, one ahead to the left and one off to the side. With the map oriented and lying flat on the ground, take a straightedge, lay it on the map with the center of the straightedge on the map landmark (Figure 2–24). Now spin the straightedge until one end points straight at the actual landmark. Draw a line across the map. Now repeat the process with the other two points. The intersection of these three lines will indicate your rough position, accurate to within one quarter mile if you were careful (Figure 2–25). Always double-check your efforts, and then carefully

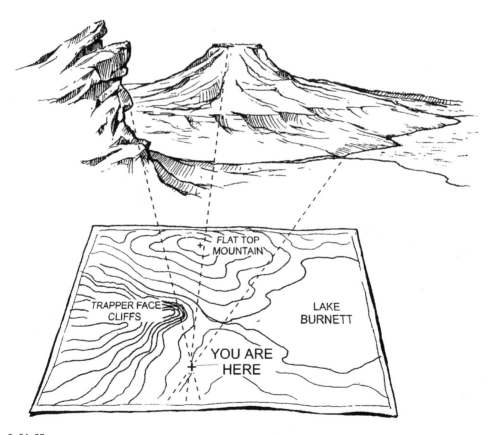

Figure 2–24, 25

compare what the map says is your approximate position with your surrounding landscape to be sure the visual information matches.

CARING FOR YOUR MAP

Waterproofing a map

There is no fun in trying to navigate while clinging to a soggy map in a downpour. Right before your eyes, the route home begins to turn into a greenish-brown papier-mâché clump. Your only hope at this point is that your memory of the route doesn't wash out like the map did.

Making a see-through, waterproof cover for your maps is an easy way to prevent soggy-map syndrome. All you need is a large, freezer-weight Ziploc bag and a few sections of sturdy, waterproof tape like duct or packing tape.

Simply cut the tape into a strip long enough to completely adhere to one edge of the bag from top to bottom. Press one-half of the tape, lengthwise, onto the side edge of the bag, leaving the other half of the tape hanging over the edge. Now flip the bag over, and fold the tape down on itself and the other side of the bag. Repeat each step twice more, once for the bottom and once for the remaining side. You now have a wonderful waterproof map container that is reinforced on three edges.

There are several other ways to waterproof a map:

- Covering a map with clear contact paper makes it waterproof but very stiff. There is no way to now write on the map with a pencil. You can, however, use an indelible ink marker to highlight your route or make notes. When done, it is possible to clean up the marks with a gauze pad soaked in rubbing alcohol.

- Paint on a product called "Stormproof" or other map water-proofing treatments by Aquaseal or Nikwax—available at most map and outdoor specialty stores. These clear chemical coatings render the map waterproof, yet it remains flexible and can be written on.

- A coating of "Thompson Water Seal" or other brick and masonry sealant will make a map water-repellent, but not waterproof.

FOLDING A MAP

Map folding is an acquired skill. Add a blowing wind, a little rain, and a sprinkling of fatigue, and what you get is an irresistible desire to jam or crumple your trail map into the nearest pocket and forget the idea of folding.

Believe it or not, there is a better way—a map folding technique that results in a very easy-to-use accordion-style configuration. It is taught to British Boy Scouts; my cousin from England can fold a map like this in his sleep.

This method allows you to look at any portion of the map without having to fully open it, which is ideal in windy or wet weather. Further, the accordion configuration collapses to pocket size with ease. Once you've established the creases, any map will fold up and down almost without effort.

Step 1 Lay the map flat, printed side up. Fold it in half vertically, with the face inside the first fold to establish the first crease. Make this and every subsequent crease clean and sharp.

Step 2 Working with only the right half of the map, fold the right side in half towards the center, resulting in one quarter-fold.

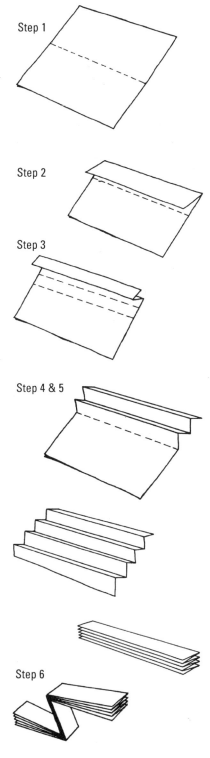

Figure 2–26

Step 3 Fold the outside quarter-fold back to the edge, producing an eighth-fold. Use this fold as a guide and fold the other quarter the same way—trust me, it's easier than it sounds.

Step 4 Half the map should now have four accordion-style folds.

Step 5 Repeat steps two and three on the map's other half so that you end up with a full accordion of eight folds in a long ruler-like shape.

Step 6 Finally, fold the map in the shape of a Z so it's in thirds. Voila! Now you can look at any section without having to completely unfold the map and it snaps into place almost by itself (Figure 2–26).

A MAP HAS ITS LIMITATIONS

Earlier, I spoke of one map limitation; some features do not show up because their elevation falls between the contour intervals. But there are other limitations to a topographic map, too—the most obvious being the man-made features shown. These were accurate only at the time the map was surveyed. New buildings may have been built and old ones torn down, new roads constructed and old ones left to deteriorate, new trails built and old ones left to return to the land. Never ever fall into the trap of resting your navigational hopes on man-made features.

Consider, too, that because the map can provide only so much information, a complete picture of how easy or difficult the terrain is to negotiate may not be evident until you are actually attempting to navigate your way through it. A number of years back, while mountaineering in the Wind River Range of Wyoming, my partner and I easily worked our way up what had appeared on the map to be a slope of such extreme steepness that we would need ropes to scale it. Upon arriving at the base, we found the slope to be steep, but covered with a layer of stable scree bisected by a wildlife trail snaking its way to the top. We followed it without difficulty.

Many are the times that I have encountered boulder fields too massive and unstable to cross safely, even though the map indicated a relatively gentle contour interval. Deep sand that sucked the life out of my legs, pea-sized gravel that made walking an adventure similar to wandering across a concrete floor covered with ball bearings, and deep muck under a layer of grass where a wonderful open meadow was supposed to exist are just a few of the adventures I have experienced—all reminders that what the map says and what reality dictates exist often on two completely different planes.

Finally, even with the best map, complete with the most assuredly accurate information, it is virtually impossible to navigate through regions that are heavily treed, or shrouded in darkness, or blessed with feature after feature that appear to be similar (as in deserts, prairies, and snowfields). For this kind of navigational situation, you must add a compass.

Chapter Three

Keep from Spinning in Circles . . . Use a Compass

- Choosing a Compass
- Types of Compasses Most Useful to the Recreationist
- Making a Compass
- Natural Navigation in the Backcountry
- Getting from Here to There
- Walking a Straight Line
- Navigating When There Aren't Landmarks
- Using the Night Sky
- Using a Watch to Tell Direction
- Let the Shadows Point the Way
- Working Your Way around Obstacles
- Caring for Your Compass

CHOOSING A COMPASS

What's the best compass for you?

That depends on the intended end use and how much money you wish to spend. The four most common brands of compass are Brunton, Nexus, Silva, and Suunto. Each company offers numerous models, each with a specific purpose and different features, but all with essentially the same role—to help an individual determine direction, plot a course, and stay on it.

As a minimum, a compass should feature a rotating bezel with a 360-degree dial in 2-degree graduations, a clear baseplate with inch and millimeter scales, a direction-of-travel arrow engraved into the baseplate, and a rotating magnetic needle mounted in a clear capsule filled with liquid to reduce shake and movement. Orienting lines should also be engraved or printed onto the bottom of the rotating capsule. A basic compass will cost around $10 with price increases relative to the number of extra features offered.

Additional features, such as a sighting mirror, built-in adjustable declination, clinometers, and/or a magnifying glass will add to the cost. For maximum accuracy, you will want a compass with a sighting mirror (often referred to as a "prismatic" type compass), which allows you to hold the compass at eye level, line up the landmark in the notched sight at the top of the mirror, and read the compass bearing using the mirror. The accuracy level of sighting goes from approximately 5 degrees of error using a simple baseplate compass to approximately 2 degrees of error or better with a mirror.

Do you really need a compass that adjusts for declination?

The difference between the true north shown on a topographic map and the magnetic north indicated by the needle on a compass is known as the declination. Declination is either west or east depending on which side of true or geographical north the compass needle points. On USGS topographic maps, declination is indicated by arrows printed on the bottom margin of the map. The arrow with a star above it indicates true or geographical north. The shorter arrow with an MN above it indicates magnetic north. If the MN arrow is on the left side of the of the true north arrow, declination is west and you will add the indicated degree amount to correct your bearing (Figure 3–1). If the MN arrow is on the right side of the true north arrow, declination is east and you will subtract the indicated degree amount to correct your bearing. While it is easy enough to do this manually (depending on your math proficiency), a compass that features a built-in declination adjustment allows you to turn a screw or adjust the housing so the compass will read true. You just have to remember that each time declination changes, often from map to map, you need to manually adjust the compass to the new setting.

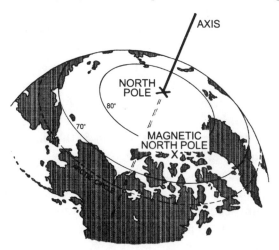

Figure 3–1

What the heck is a clinometer and why would I need one?

A clinometer is used to measure vertical angles or the slope of hills or other objects and is especially useful if you are planning to do any serious snowshoeing, backcountry skiing, or winter mountaineering where avalanches might become a concern. With a clinometer, you will be able to accurately estimate the steepness of terrain and determine the degree of risk of avalanche danger. Other than winter use, however, a clinometer doesn't offer much for the recreational user other than a way to determine slope angle and be able to say, "We hiked up a 45-degree slope . . . wahooo!"

More Lingo—Understanding Compass Speak

- **Azimuth Ring (or Housing):** The circular housing with textured edges that rotates on the compass base for taking or setting bearings. Degree markings, from zero to 360, are typically etched into its surface making up the Azimuth Ring or Graduated Dial, and it is often liquid-filled (Figure 3–2).

- **Gun Type Sights:** Most often found on prismatic (sighting) compasses, these sights are used like those on a gun for sighting and taking bearings with maximum accuracy (Figure 3–2).

- **Index Line:** The mark on the front of the sight or compass baseplate where you read the indicated bearing (Figure 3–2).

- **Line-of-Travel or Direction-of-Travel Arrow:** A line or arrow engraved on the baseplate of your compass that points you in the direction you need to go to get to your desired destination (Figure 3–2).

- **Liquid Damping:** Liquid damping allows the needle to come to a rest rapidly and helps to hold the needle steady, allowing for faster and more accurate readings. Compasses that do not have liquid damping leave the user waiting for what seems like a lifetime for the needle to stop spinning, and then makes the user squint to determine which point the bouncy needle is actually pointing to. The better compasses use a kerosene-based fluid or some other additive to ensure the liquid does not freeze or boil from minus 40 F to plus 120 F (Figure 3–2).

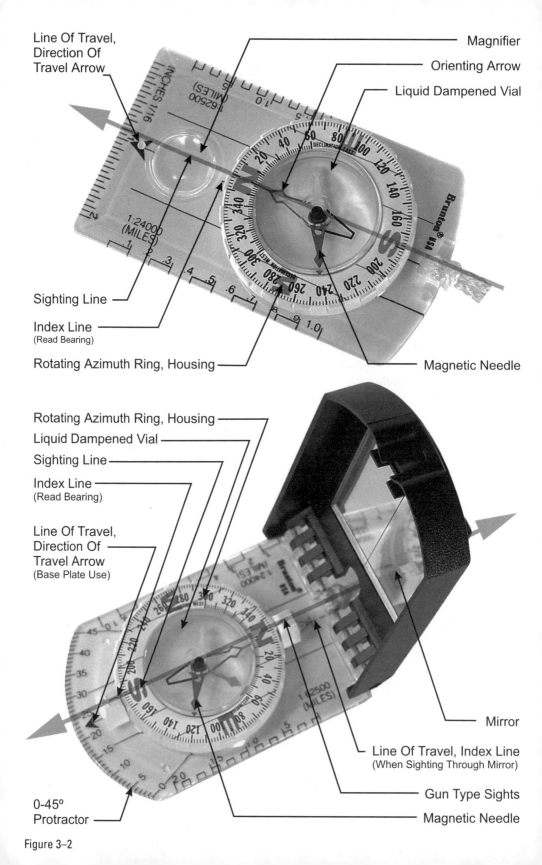

Line Of Travel, Direction Of Travel Arrow

Magnifier

Orienting Arrow

Liquid Dampened Vial

Sighting Line

Index Line
(Read Bearing)

Rotating Azimuth Ring, Housing

Magnetic Needle

Rotating Azimuth Ring, Housing

Liquid Dampened Vial

Sighting Line

Index Line
(Read Bearing)

Line Of Travel, Direction Of Travel Arrow
(Base Plate Use)

Mirror

Line Of Travel, Index Line
(When Sighting Through Mirror)

Gun Type Sights

Magnetic Needle

0-45° Protractor

Figure 3–2

- **Magnifier:** The sole purpose of this feature is to assist you in reading the oftentimes extremely small print on a map (Figure 3–2).

- **Mirror:** Incorporated into a hard-case lid that folds down over the top of the compass housing, the mirror is used to make prismatic in-line sightings, the most accurate method of using a hand-held compass. The prismatic compass allows you to hold the compass at eye level, sighting both the distant object through the gun sight and the compass face at the same time (Figure 3–2).

- **Orienting Arrow:** This is the outlined arrow engraved into the base of your compass housing and often lined with red paint. The arrow is made to exactly outline the outside of the magnetic needle. By centering or "boxing" the magnetic needle within the orienting arrow's outline, both pointing in the same direction (unless back-sighting), you are able to determine your bearing or direction of travel (Figure 3–2).

- **Protractor:** Some models have a feature that allows you to more easily plot a bearing on a map (Figure 3–2).

- **Sighting Line:** This is the line you sight along on a hand-held compass to take a bearing (Figure 3–2).

TYPES OF COMPASSES MOST USEFUL TO THE RECREATIONIST

While each company has its own particular idiosyncrasies relative to features, the following generalizations run fairly true across the board for compass-type descriptions:

- Simple (starter type) compasses: Usually feature 5-degree increments, orienting arrows, and simple map measuring scales (Figure 3–3).   Figure 3–3

Figure 3–4

Figure 3–5

Figure 3–6

- Basic Baseplate Compasses: Usually feature 2-degree increments, orienting arrows, more detailed measuring scales, and sometimes include lanyards (Figure 3–4).

- Basic Baseplate Compasses with declination scale: Usually feature 2-degree increments, orienting arrows, more detailed measuring scales, lanyards, and built-in adjustable declination correction scales. Sometimes include magnifying glass and nighttime glow-in-the-dark markings (Figure 3–5).

- Mirror/Sighting Compasses: Usually feature 2-degree increments, orienting arrows, more detailed measuring scales, lanyards, fixed or adjustable declination correction scales, and sighting mirrors. Sometimes include magnifying glass and nighttime glow-in-the-dark markings. Up to 1-degree accuracy of scale when sighting (Figure 3–6).

- Orienteering/Competition Compasses: Usually feature 2-degree increments, orienting arrows,

very detailed measuring
scales (sometimes inter-
changeable), adjustable
declination correction
scales, anti-slip rubber
pads, magnifying glass-
es, a heavier needle and
special dampening fluid
for quicker readings,
map templates for
marking controls, and
lanyards. Sometimes

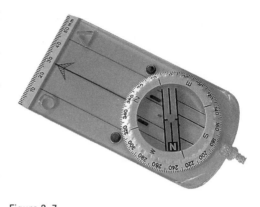

Figure 3–7

include a clinometer (Figure 3–7).

- Sighting Compasses: Usually feature 1-degree increments,
optics, and accuracy of scale to .5 degrees. Sometimes electronic,
these units are primarily intended for professional use when
accuracy to the nth degree is critical. The Brunton Pocket Transit
and Pro-Line Outdoorsman Series fall into this category. While
recreationists can and do use this type of compass, these
compasses don't have a baseplate and consequently they are not
as easily used with a map. These compasses are best suited for
those times when route-finding will be done by compass alone
(Figure 3–8).

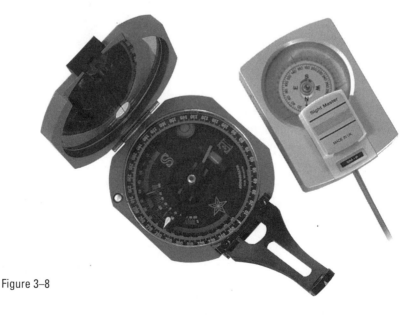

Figure 3–8

Matching Intended Use to Compass

Compass Type	Hiking / Fishing	Off-Trail / Mountaineering	General/ Scouts	Orienteering/ Competition	Professional
Simple (starter type)	yes	no	yes	no	no
Basic Baseplate	yes	no	yes	yes	no
Basic Baseplate w/ declination scale	yes	yes	yes	yes	no
Mirror/Sighting	yes	yes	yes	yes	yes
Orienteering	no	no	no	yes	no
Sighting	no	yes	no	no	yes

Other Compass Types

The compasses listed above are, in my opinion, the best choices for the recreational user. There are, however, several other types you are likely to encounter.

Figure 3–9

- Fixed Dial Compasses: Fixed dial compasses are affixed to watchbands, knife handles, zipper pull tabs, and are sold as very simple hand-held compasses, too. They will feature a molded plastic case, typically with 5-degree increments engraved onto it. They have no baseplate, no way of adjusting for declination short of mathematical calculation and are basically useless for anything more than simple compass-only route-finding applications (Figure 3–9).

- Military-style Lensatic Compasses: Since these compasses get sold through military surplus stores and numerous discount warehouses, they are popular. They come with a forward and rear sight and a lens with a line in it used to read and establish a bearing. Since this compass has no baseplate, it is very difficult to use effectively with a map, and it's claim of improved accuracy over a mirrored sighting compass is debatable at best (Figure 3–10).

MAKING A COMPASS

Figure 3–10

Nothing will help you to understand how a compass works like making one. Learning the principals is useful, too, if you should ever find yourself having to rig a compass, performing a MacGyveresque improvisation (after the TV character who specializes in fashioning technological tools out of mere scraps). School children the world over have made compasses out of a needle and cork, and the following tutorial is right out of the pages of almost any fifth grade science text.

Take a non-metal container such as a cup or a bowl and fill it with water. Take a wine bottle cork and slice a half-inch thick section off the narrower end. Suspend a steel needle in the water by sticking it through the top third of the cork, so that when the cork is placed in the water, the unit floats with needle remaining clear of the water. Stroke the sharp end of the needle repeatedly and in the same direction with a magnet. The magnetized end of the needle will now point towards magnetic north. You may have to re-magnetize the needle every so often.

So how does this help you in a survival situation? Keep in mind that every radio, including those found in vehicles, utilize a magnet as part of the speaker. Don't have a cork? So find a twig or a wooden matchstick or anything else that will float freely. No non-metallic container for water, or no water at all? Don't fret. Hang the needle from a very fine thread, making sure that it is not twisted. No needle? Anything metal will suffice, including small nails, pins, or the edge of a razor-blade—it just has to be made of metal that can be magnetized. In doubt as to whether the metal you are using can be magnetized? Try picking it up with the magnet. If the magnet attracts the metal, you can magnetize it.

For those of you who are really in an experimental mood, you can magnetize a needle or nail or another strip of metal with nothing more than insulated copper wire (found inside most radios or other types of electrical gear) and a battery that generates at least six volts of charge. Wrap a length of insulated copper wire around the metal approximately twenty-five to forty times. Connect each end of the wire to your battery's terminals. It takes about twenty-five to forty-five minutes to effectively magnetize the metal. When the time is up, suspend the magnetized metal as indicated in the paragraphs above. The end that points towards north will be the end that was nearest the negative (-) terminal on the battery—N for Negative or North. My science teacher loved this experiment—sometimes, I think, a little too much!

NATURAL NAVIGATION IN THE BACKCOUNTRY

Staying on course when stepping a lively beat down a trail is relatively simple; just stay alert, follow the trail, and read the signs. Off trail, especially on snow fields, ice flows, and desert sands, route-finding is an entirely different beast. A compass is an invaluable aid, but so is an observant eye. When miles and miles of trackless terrain exists, taking note of the prevailing wind direction and the resulting textures it leaves on the land offer essential information. On tundra and sea ice in the Arctic, systematic drift patterns in the snow—sastrugi—offer a valuable directional clue. Use a compass to check on the directional formations of these patterns and then remember them. The same is true of sand drifts in desert environments. Taking note of these physical directional clues becomes invaluable if a sandstorm or snowstorm whips up that limits visibility and impairs the taking of distant compass bearing points. In conditions of such limited visibility you can use sand drifts and sastrugi underfoot to aid in staying on track and to keep from wandering endlessly in circles.

Other natural clues can also aid in staying your course. On the ocean's coast, for example, or on any other large body of water, prevailing winds will typically blow offshore during the morning hours and back onshore as the sun sets—a result of the heating and then cooling of the earth inland.

Forget the old adage "moss grows on the north side of a tree." Moss grows wherever it is cool and damp. Most frequently, this is either on the north or south side of a tree, the sides that receive the least amount of sun throughout a day.

GETTING FROM HERE TO THERE

One of the most valuable things about a compass is that it will assist you in getting from point A to point B, even if you lose sight of B along the way. How? Begin by taking a bearing. Say what? You take a bearing by first holding the compass level and pointing the direction-of-travel arrow directly at the landmark you want to head towards. With the direction-of-travel arrow pointed at the landmark, point B, turn the housing until the orienting arrow points the same way and boxes (surrounds) the floating magnetic needle. Now read the degree of heading indicated on the housing and adjacent to the index point. This degree reading is your heading. As you hike off from point A and descend into the woods, all you have to do is keep walking in the same direction indicated by the direction-of-travel arrow when the magnetic needle is boxed by the orienting arrow and the housing is turned to place the established degree bearing at the index point. Simple?

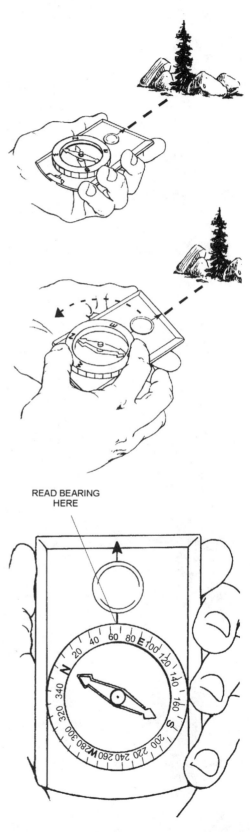

READ BEARING HERE

Figure 3–11 **Taking A Bearing**. Hold compass level with direction-of-travel arrow pointing towards a landmark. Rotate housing and "box" magnetic needle with orienting arrow. Read bearing at index line.

Yes, and no. Even if you walk for miles in the direction indicated by your compass, you can still end up vastly off course. How? By drifting right or left as you walk, a very common mistake (Figure 3–11).

WALKING A STRAIGHT LINE

You can correct for drift and ensure that you always walk a straight line from point A to point B by navigating from point to point along the way. Once you have established your bearing, sight along the direction-of-travel arrow and establish an intermediate landmark—one you will not lose sight of along the way—and hike directly towards it. Once there, sight along your compass again, being sure it is set to the correct heading, and establish another landmark to hike towards. In this way, you will hike point-to-point all the way to point B in as straight a line as possible (Figure 3–12).

If you ever have any doubt as to your chosen route of travel (it is possible to arrive at your intermediate landmark and wonder if the boulder or tree or peak you are on is the correct landmark when another similar looking landmark exists nearby) take a back sighting. You do this by turning around and facing your point of origin, assuming it is still visible, or your last established and still identifiable landmark. Point your direction-of-travel arrow directly at the landmark and center (box) the magnetic needle with the orienting arrow, only this time the needle and the arrow will point in opposite directions. If you cannot center (box) the needle, don't move the

Figure 3–12

housing. Instead, move to the right or the left until you can center (box) the needle by repointing the direction-of-travel arrow. Now you are back on course.

Learning to establish a back bearing is very useful if you decide to cut your trip short for any reason and head back to point A, your point of origin. Once the needle is boxed, rotate the housing until both the magnetic needle and orienting arrow are pointing the same way. Now, read the new degree bearing at the index point. You can achieve the same effect by performing a little math as well. If your original heading was 180 degrees (due south), then a back bearing or return trip would be 360 degrees (due north). The formula for this is: for bearings greater than 180, subtract 180 degrees to arrive at the correct return bearing; for bearings less than 180, add 180 degrees to arrive at the correct return bearing. For example, an original bearing of 30 degrees from point A to point B would mean a return bearing of 210 degrees from point B to point A. Or, an original bearing of 220 degrees from point A to point B would mean a return bearing of 40 degrees from point B to point A. Make sense? Kinda makes you wish you had paid more attention to Mr. Frumplemeyer when he was outlining those math formulas in ninth grade now doesn't it (Figure 3–13)?

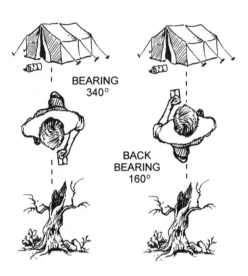

BEARING
340°

BACK
BEARING
160°

Figure 3–13

NAVIGATING WHEN THERE AREN'T LANDMARKS

There will be times when landmarks disappear beneath a shroud of fog, or are masked by a dense forest, or disappear altogether as you make your way across a featureless plain, a snowfield, or a desert. Working your way along a course under these conditions is

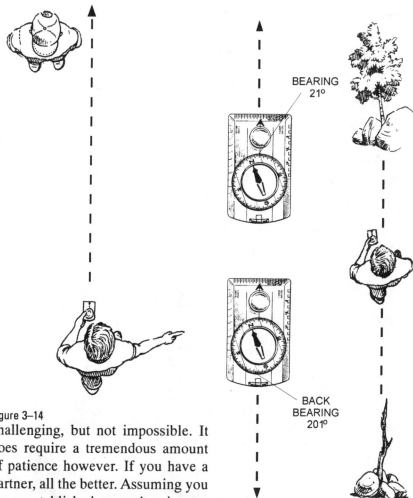

Figure 3–14

BEARING 21°

BACK BEARING 201°

Figure 3–15

challenging, but not impossible. It does require a tremendous amount of patience however. If you have a partner, all the better. Assuming you have established your bearing as indicated above, you will use your partner as the intermediate landmark. Point your direction-of-travel arrow ahead and have your hiking partner head off in that direction. Stay in visual contact at all times. Before your partner disappears from sight, have him or her stop and turn around to face you. It is essential you line them up exactly in line with the imaginary beam the direction-of-travel arrow is sending toward the invisible landmark. Move them to the right or left with hand signals until they are exactly in place. Now hike towards them (Figure 3–14).

What happens if you are alone? It gets more difficult, though not impossible. Get ready to backsight like mad. Before heading off along the bearing indicated by your direction-of-travel arrow, erect a visible monument at the point you are now standing. It can be a large branch propped up so it is visible from a distance, or several rocks stacked one on top of the other—it doesn't matter so long as it is visible and natural. Don't needlessly mar the landscape. Hike off from your landmark, stopping just before you lose sight of it. Take a backbearing and place yourself on course by moving right or left until your magnetic needle is boxed by the orienting arrow and the direction-of-travel arrow is pointing exactly at your monument. Turn around, set up another monument to your travels, and head off again. It will take you a while, but you'll eventually get to where you want to go (Figure 3–15).

USING THE NIGHT SKY

Celestial Navigation Using the North Star

Yes, navigating by Polaris (also known as the North Star) does require a clear view of the sky and an ability to identify at least one star formation—the Big Dipper—but, assuming you can pick out the Big Dipper, you can determine which way is north. The beauty of the North Star is that it stays in one place in the sky and is always to the north of you. To pick

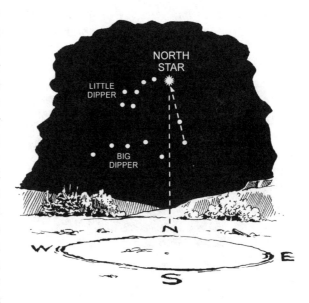

Figure 3–16

it out of the mass of other twinkling stars, find the Big Dipper, then look to the two stars that make up the lip of the dipper's ladle. The North Star lies above those two stars, known as pointer stars, in a relatively straight line, approximately four to six times the distance between the two stars.

How does this help you? Well, if you consider that a compass is nothing more than a circle with north at the top, south at the bottom, east to the right and west to the left, you can draw a crude circle in the soil and mark off the cardinal reference points (N, S, E, W) based on the north end of the circle pointing directly at the North Star (Figure 3–16).

If you have a map, you can now orient it fairly accurately and get a good read of the land. Don't have a map? Whoops! Don't panic though. You can still navigate by using the North Star to maintain your sense of direction and prevent yourself from hiking in circles, wasting valuable time and energy.

What about Celestial Navigation in the Southern Hemisphere?

Unfortunately, it isn't as easy as in the Northern Hemisphere, chiefly because there is no clearly visible star whose position remains firmly

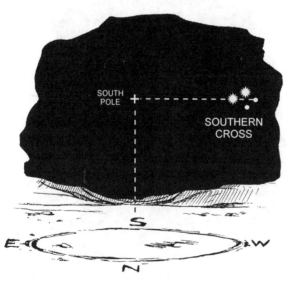

Figure 3–17

fixed in the sky, like the North Star. Still, it is possible, using a little careful estimation and visualization, to navigate by the stars. First of all, you must locate the Southern Cross. The upright of the cross, or the longest section is made up of four clearly visible stars, with a fifth, much fainter star resting just off center. If your eyes can follow a line through this longer section of the cross to a point approximately four and a half times its length, you will arrive at a point where a "South Star" would be if it existed. Find a landmark directly below this point and that will become your south reference point.

Create a roughly drawn compass in the soil, as indicated above, so that when the sun rises, you will still be able to determine which way is south and then, hopefully, which way you should be heading (Figure 3–17).

USING A WATCH TO TELL DIRECTION

Northern Hemisphere

Even if you don't have a watch, you can get a good sense of direction established, providing you can see the sun. I've determined the sun's position, even on a hazy day, by being able to locate the glowing orb hidden behind a veil of clouds. If you are wearing a watch with an hour hand, and you are sure your watch is set to the correct local time, then the going is simple. By holding the watch level, turn yourself until the hour hand points in the direction of the sun. Establish a point on your watch that is one-half the distance between the hour hand and

12. The north/south line runs from this point half-way between the hour hand and 12 and the center of the watch. North is the point on the line furthest from the sun (Figure 3–18).

Not wearing a watch, or your watch is digital? No worries mate, as long as you have a relatively good imagination and are absolutely sure of the time. Imagine you are wearing a watch and place the hour hand in the correct position for the time of day. Now follow the directions as indicated in the paragraph above and you will find yourself facing in the same direction. Keep in mind that the watch method is not 100 percent

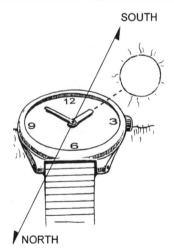

Figure 3–18 This illustration is for Northern Hemisphere use. For the Southern Hemisphere switch north and south on the arrow, and point noon at the sun.

accurate, but it will offer a good enough fix to offer navigational aid to an outdoorsperson.

Southern Hemisphere

If you are south of the equator, and your watch is again set to the correct local time, you will vary the technique somewhat by aiming noon or the number 12 directly at the sun. Establish a point on the watch face that is half-way between 12 and the hour hand. The north/south line runs from that point directly through the center of the watch. North will be indicated by the point on the line that is closest to the sun.

Figure 3–19

LET THE SHADOWS POINT THE WAY

Did you ever attempt to make a sun dial when you were a child? Telling the time relied on the creation of a good shadow from a bright sun. Well, determining east and west from shadows cast by the sun is no different really—you need a bright sun and a large enough stick to create a good shadow.

Push a straight stick into the ground in as vertical a position as possible. Place a pebble or scratch a mark at the end point where the shadow is cast. Now, if you have a watch, time about thirty minutes. Without a watch, spend your minutes counting out half-an-hour: one-1,000, two-1,000, etc. After approximately thirty minutes have passed, place another pebble or scratch another mark at the second end point where the shadow is cast.

Now, draw a straight line connecting the two points. This line is pointing approximately east/west with west indicated by the first positioned rock and east the second (Figure 3–19).

WORKING YOUR WAY AROUND OBSTACLES

What happens if you come to a natural obstacle you hadn't counted on, an obstacle that stands directly in your path and established compass bearing? No problem! The easiest method is to select a landmark on the other side of the obstacle—assuming that your obstacle is something flat such as a lake or a wide swamp. Work your way around the lake to the landmark, take a backsighting to be sure you are actually back on course, and then proceed. However, if the obstacle is a massive cliff and there is no way to establish a visible landmark on the other side in line with your established route of travel, you must opt for option two. Hike around it, using measured steps and maintaining a calculated bearing and keeping your changes in course as close to absolute right angle (90 degree) turns as possible.

Once you arrive at the obstacle, keep the compass direction-of-travel arrow pointing at your intended direction, but turn and face to

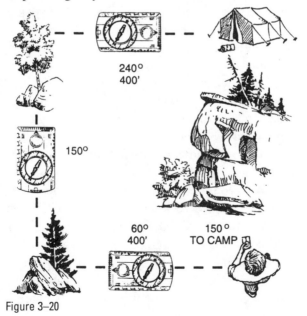

240°
400'

150°

60°
400'

150°
TO CAMP

Figure 3–20

the right or left. You should now be holding the compass so that you are able to sight along its back edge, with the direction-of-travel arrow pointing directly off toward your right or left. Walk as straight a line as possible toward a distant landmark established by sighting off of the back edge of the baseplate. Walk carefully and count your steps exactly. Once you are at a point where you are around the obstacle and can resume heading in the correct direction, turn and resume walking in line with your compass's direction-of-travel arrow. Keep in mind, however, that you are now off course, although heading in the correct direction. To get back on course, you will need to head back in the opposite direction once you are around the obstacle. To do this, again turn your body so that you are able to sight along the back edge of the baseplate and establish a landmark to hike towards. Now, hike in a straight line, counting steps again. Stop hiking when you have walked exactly the number of steps you counted before. At this point, turn back in line with your compass's direction-of-travel arrow and resume hiking, now not only in the correct direction, but back on course.

CARING FOR YOUR COMPASS

Although your compass is built to take a licking and keep on pointing, a little TLC for your navigational friend is in good order and well advised. For starters, try not to drop it or let it bang against hard surfaces—if you let a compass hang loosely around your neck from a lanyard, it's liable to whack against hard objects which do it no good. I tuck my compass inside my shirt to protect it when it is hanging around my neck and not in use. If you have a sighting compass with a cover, keep it closed when not in use. I would also recommend that you purchase a nylon or leather sheath for your compass for additional protection when carrying it in a pack or pocket.

Never leave your compass sitting in an extremely hot environment, such as on a rock under intense desert sun or on the dashboard or in the glove compartment of your car. Extreme temperatures can cause the damping fluid in your compass to rupture the housing and leak out, rendering your compass useless.

Keep your compass away from high-intensity magnetic fields, such as electromagnets (electric motors as an example), as they can temporarily disoriented or even permanently demagnetize the compass's needle. Your compass won't be much good to you if the formerly magnetized needle wanders aimlessly just when you are counting on it to point you in the right direction.

While using repellents is often essential to thwart the attacks of mosquitoes, black flies, midges, and ticks, the chemicals in repellents (most typically DEET) can, and most often will, eat the ink right off your compass's housing. Worse, DEET has been known to affect the plastic housing of a compass causing it to cloud up and even crack—a major bummer. Be sure to clean your hands thoroughly before touching your compass.

Over time, the needle on your compass may begin to act sluggishly; it may even appear to stick to the bottom of the liquid-filled housing. Most often, this is due to a build up of static electricity within the housing and can be corrected by simply rubbing a small amount of water directly over the housing to disburse the static charge.

It is not uncommon for a small bubble to appear in the liquid-filled housing when you are using your compass in high elevations or in temperatures below freezing. The bubble forms because the fluid within the housing contracts or expands at a faster rate than the housing, resulting in a "vacuum" bubble. This bubble will not affect the performance of your compass as the liquid's sole purpose is to dampen or slow down the movement of the magnetic needle. Typically, any bubble will disappear when the compass is returned to room temperature and/or lower elevation. If the bubble remains, it is possible to correct the situation by placing the compass in a warm (not hot) spot, such as a sunny window sill. Do keep an eye on the bubble if it refuses to depart. Should the bubble grow in size, you might have a small, almost imperceptible leak in the liquid-filled compass housing, and that means you need a new compass.

Chapter Four

Making the Compass and Map Work for You

- Orienting Your Map
- Orienting the Map to Magnetic North; Projecting Magnetic Lines
- Orienting the Map to Magnetic North; Use Your Compass's Declination Adjustment
- Orienting the Map and Adjusting For Declination by Adding or Subtracting
- How Do I Take a Field Bearing?
- How Do I Take a Map Bearing?
- It's on the Map; How Do I Find It in the Field?
- It's in the Field; How Do I Find It on the Map?
- Establishing Bearings without Orienting the Map
- Minimizing Mistakes

ORIENTING YOUR MAP

Since a map represents the lay of the land, you must accurately orient your map to the lay of the land if you wish to match the geographical picture with the map image. You can do this by picking out landmarks and then spinning your map to match those landmarks—assuming your map reading skills and your geographical interpretation skills are good enough. Still, geographic orientation is only roughly accurate, even with the best observation. For absolute accuracy, you will need to turn to your compass which will help you orient the map so it becomes an exact mirror image of the terrain around you. Since the map is printed with the edges lined up with true north and your compass's needle always points toward magnetic north, you will have to account for declination to correctly align your map.

As I have discussed in the previous chapters, the difference between north shown on a topographic map and the north indicated by the magnetic needle on your compass is known as declination. Declination is either west or east depending on which side of geographical north the compass needle points. On USGS topographic maps, declination is indicated by arrows printed on the bottom margin of the map. The arrow with a star above it indicates

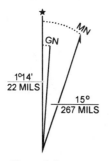

Figure 4–1

true or geographical north. The shorter arrow with an MN above it indicates magnetic north. The number with the degree sign printed between the two arrows is the exact degree of declination (Figure 4–1; see also Appendix Figure A–4, page 138).

There are several ways to ensure accuracy. First, you can orient the map simply by drawing magnetic lines across the map that parallel the declination angle (in essence, you're adjusting the map to magnetic compass-speak). This is my favorite method since once the magnetic lines are drawn, your compass's magnetic needle, its orienting arrow, and the map will all be speaking the same language, minimizing the possibility for field errors. The disadvantage of this method is that you have to draw magnetic lines across all of the maps you plan to use in the field, and you must draw them very accurately using a protractor, a perfectly straight yardstick, and a relatively flat surface. In my opinion, the next best method, and a very close second to the first, is adjusting your compass to the declination indicated on the map (this time adjusting the compass to geographic/true north map-speak). The advantage of this method is that once your compass is adjusted, assuming you have a built-in declination adjustment feature, which is worth the few extra dollars you will spend to get it, you can forget about having to compensate for declination as long as you remain on that map. All you have to do is turn a screw, spin a dial or adjust a scale—no drawing lines whatsoever. The disadvantage is that you will have to remember to adjust your setting when moving to adjacent maps with possibly different declinations—a very minor disadvantage to be sure. The third method involves the magic of numbers and mathematical calculation the declination—not just when orienting the map, but when taking bearings from the map or from the field. If you are to be a well-rounded and skilled navigator, it is essential you understand this method, although I personally hate it and rarely rely on it. Why? Because when you are fatigued, stressed, anxious, or hurried, numbers add a distraction that can become quite confusing, dramatically increasing the possibility of error.

ORIENTING THE MAP TO MAGNETIC NORTH; PROJECTING MAGNETIC LINES

A common way to make the process of adjusting for declination easy is to use a protractor, a yard-stick with a very straight edge, and a pencil to project the declination line across the entire topo. Your first step is to mark a point along the bottom border of the map and then place the center point of the pro-tractor directly on your mark. Make another mark at the degree bear-ing indicated by the

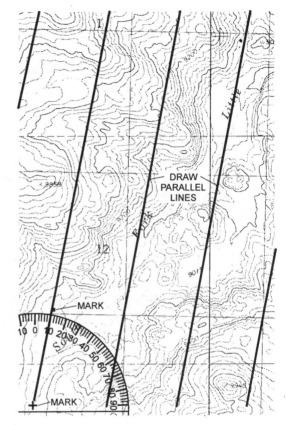

Figure 4–2

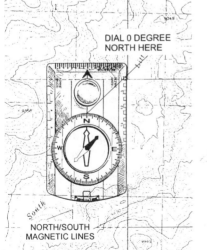

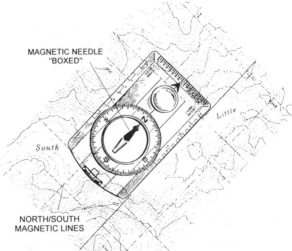

Figure 4–3 **Orienting A Map with Magnetic Lines.** Dial zero degree North into the direction-of-travel arrow (index line). Place edge of compass on drawn magnetic lines. Without moving the compass, rotate map until magnetic needle is "boxed" with orienting arrow.

declination angle, being sure that your angle is facing the same way as the declination diagram. For example, a 10-degree declination to the east (the MN arrow is to the right of the arrow with the star above it, will mean that you will count 10 degrees to the right of the zero-degree marking on the protractor, placing a mark at 10 degrees. Now, connect the two points and project the line all the way across the map using the yardstick. Finally, using this line as a guide, you can draw parallel magnetic-north lines one to two inches apart (Figure 4–2). Now, take the compass with the orienting arrow pointing due north, place the edge of the baseplate along one of the magnetic lines and spin the map until the magnetic arrow is centered (boxed) within the orienting arrow (Figure 4–3).

ORIENTING THE MAP TO MAGNETIC NORTH; USE YOUR COMPASS'S DECLINATION ADJUSTMENT

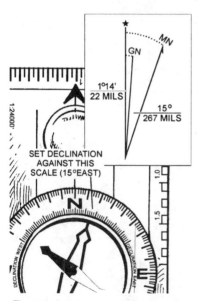

Figure 4–4

No magnetic lines on your map? Then the next easiest method is to adjust your compass to the declination, which is easy if your compass features a built-in declination adjustment. Each manufacturer has a different method to accomplish this, so it is best to refer to the instructions that come with your compass. All methods accomplish the same thing, however. By moving the orienting arrow to the right of north for east declination or to the left of north for west declination, the compass will read true or geographic north (Figure 4–4). To orient the map, place the edge of the compass's baseplate along the printed edge of the map, and then spin the map until the red end of the magnetic needle is centered (boxed) in the orienting arrow. Your map is now oriented to magnetic north. You will note that the north/south line of your compass and the direction-of-travel arrow parallel the edge of

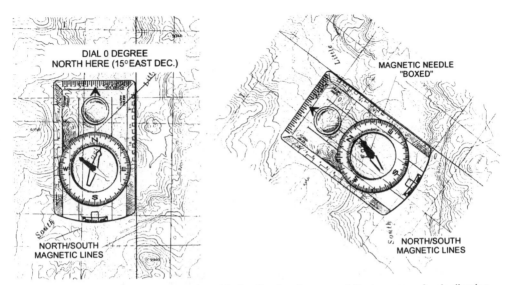

Figure 4–5 **Orienting a Map with an Adjustable Declination Compass.** Adjust compass for declination, dialing zero degree North with the direction-of-travel arrow (index line). Place compass along north/south line on map. Without moving the compass, rotate map until magnetic needle is "boxed" with orienting arrow.

your map indicating true north, while the magnetic needle continues to point east or west, matching the angle of declination indicated by the map's declination diagram—nifty isn't it? Once your compass is set, you won't have to readjust the declination as long as you are navigating within the boundaries of that map. Don't forget, however, that as you move from map to map and region to region, the declination will change and you will have to adjust the compass accordingly each time (Figure 4–5).

ORIENTING THE MAP AND ADJUSTING FOR DECLINATION BY ADDING OR SUBTRACTING

If you do not have a compass that features a built-in declination adjustment, you will have to resort to turning the compass housing to compensate for the declination before each attempt to orient your map. If the MN arrow is on the left side of the true north arrow, declination is west and you will turn the housing to the left (counterclockwise), counting each degree until north sits the designated number of degrees of declination to the right of the index point (10 degrees of west declination means you will turn the housing until 10 degrees is indicated opposite the compass's index point: 360 degrees (north) + 10 degrees = 10 degrees. How did I get 10 degrees by adding 10 to 360? Remember that a compass is a 360-degree circle. You can't go higher than 360 degrees, no matter how hard you try. So, when adding to 360 degrees, you are, in actual fact, adding to zero degrees and continuing around the circle to the right. If the MN arrow is on the right side of the true north arrow, declination is east and you will turn the housing to the right (clockwise), counting each degree until north sits the designated number of degrees of declination to the left of the index point (10 degrees of east declination means you will turn the housing until 350 degrees is indicated opposite the compass's index point: 360 degrees (north) − 10 degrees = 350 degrees (Figure 4–6).

Should you opt for this method, realize that you aren't done with Math 101 just because your map is successfully oriented. Any time you take a bearing from the map to the compass or field or from the compass

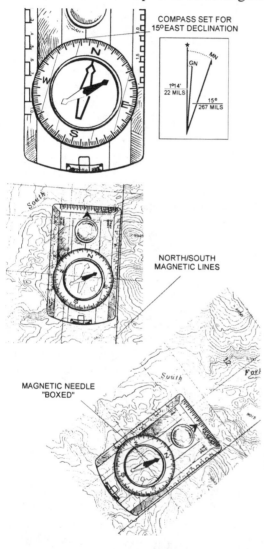

COMPASS SET FOR 15°EAST DECLINATION

NORTH/SOUTH MAGNETIC LINES

MAGNETIC NEEDLE "BOXED"

Figure 4–6 **Orienting Map.** Dial zero degree North into direction-of-travel arrow. Place compass along north/south line on map. Without moving the compass, rotate housing and "box" magnetic needle with orienting arrow. Adjust for declination error.

or field to the map, you will have to convert the reading so that it compensates for declination. How?

To compensate for declination when taking a reading from the map that you want to use in the field, you will need to do the following: If the MN arrow is on the left side of the of the true north arrow, declination is west and you will add the indicated degree amount to correct your bearing. If the MN arrow is on the right side of the true north arrow, declination is east and you will subtract the indicated degree amount to correct your bearing.

To compensate for declination when taking a reading from the field that you want to use on the map, you will need to do the following: If the MN arrow is on the left side of the true north arrow, declination is west and you will subtract the indicated degree amount to correct your bearing. If the MN arrow is on the right side of the true north arrow, declination is east and you will add the indicated degree amount to correct your bearing (Figure 4–7).

Say what? It's really not as hard as it sounds. If your indicated heading is 80 degrees after taking a map bearing, and the map declination is 10 degrees east, you will turn your bezel 10 degrees east, subtracting the degrees, to leave you with a corrected bearing of 70 degrees.

Why is this important? In this example, if you did not correct for declination and set off hiking on an 80 degree bearing, you would be off course by approximately one-fifth of a mile for each mile traveled (for each degree off error, you'll be approximately 18 feet off course for every 1,000 feet traveled)—no wonder you can't find that fresh-water spring!

20°WEST DECLINATION

20°EAST DECLINATION

Figure 4–7 Rotate azimuth ring 15 degrees east of zero degree-North to adjust for declination. Place compass along north/south line on map. Without moving compass, rotate map until magnetic needle is "boxed" with orienting arrow.

Declination Error Example Chart

Declination Error	Distance Traveled	Distance Off Course
1 degree	1 mile	92 feet
1 degree	5 miles	460 feet
1 degree	10 miles	921 feet (approx. 1/5 mile)
2 degrees	1 mile	184 feet
2 degrees	5 miles	921 feet (approx. 1/5 mile)
2 degrees	10 miles	1,844 feet (approx. 1/3 mile)
5 degrees	1 mile	461 feet
5 degrees	5 miles	2,309 feet (approx. 1/2 mile)
5 degrees	10 miles	4,619 feet (approx. 4/5 mile)
10 degrees	1 mile	931 feet (approx. 1/5 mile)
10 degrees	5 miles	4,655 feet (approx. 4/5 mile)
10 degrees	10 miles	9,310 feet (approx. 1 3/4 miles)
20 degrees	1 mile	1,921 feet (approx. 1/3 mile)
20 degrees	5 miles	9,608 feet (approx. 1 4/5 miles)
20 degrees	10 miles	19,219 feet (approx. 3 2/3 miles)

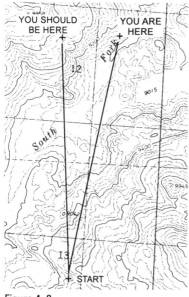

Figure 4–8

HOW DO I TAKE A FIELD BEARING?

Imagine that you are hiking toward a distant mountain peak, presently visible from the ridge you are on, but you know that you will soon lose sight of it in the woods. How can you be sure you will stay on course? Hold your compass level at waist height and point the direction-of-travel arrow at the mountain peak. Rotate the compass housing until the red end of the magnetic compass needle is centered (boxed) within the orienting arrow. Your bearing may be read in degrees at the center index point—where the compass housing meets the direction-of-travel arrow on the compass baseplate.

To follow that bearing, pick the first major landmark in line with the direction-of-travel arrow, say a large evergreen—one that you will not lose sight of once into the woods. Also, look over your shoulder and select a major landmark (say a rocky outcrop) feature directly behind you—again, one you will not lose sight of. Do not touch that compass dial! Walk directly towards the evergreen and don't worry that you can no longer see the mountain peak because your compass reading has already been set at the index. Once at the tree, hold the compass level once again, turn your body until the north end of the compass needle centers itself exactly inside the orienting arrow and then find another landmark in line with the direction-of-travel arrow. Before you head out, take a back bearing by turning around with the compass still held level until the white end of the compass needle is now centered inside the orienting arrow. Do you see the rocky outcrop in line with the direction-of-travel arrow? If so, you're on course for the mountain peak as planned. Turn around and head directly to your next selected landmark. Repeat the procedure until you arrive at your selected destination, the mountain peak (Figure 4–9).

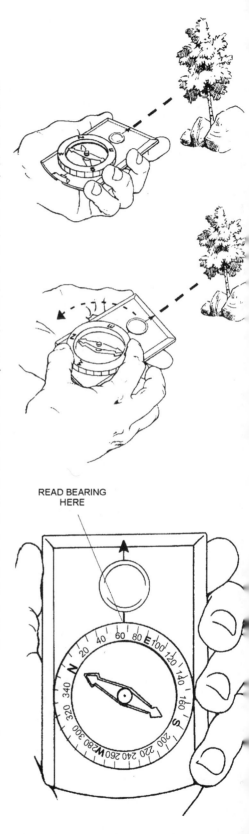

READ BEARING HERE

Figure 4–9 **Field Bearing.** Hold compass level with travel arrow pointing towards a landmark. Rotate housing and "box" magnetic needle with orienting arrow. Read bearing at index line.

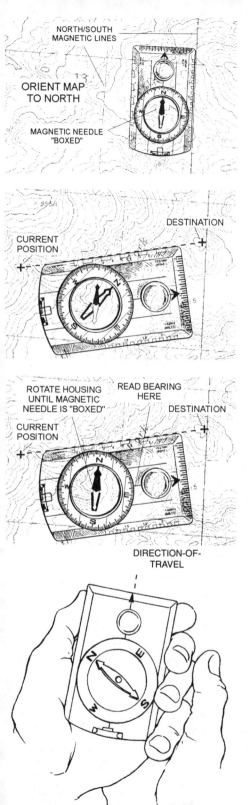

NORTH/SOUTH
MAGNETIC LINES

ORIENT MAP
TO NORTH

MAGNETIC NEEDLE
"BOXED"

DESTINATION

CURRENT
POSITION

ROTATE HOUSING   READ BEARING
UNTIL MAGNETIC   HERE
NEEDLE IS "BOXED"   DESTINATION

CURRENT
POSITION

DIRECTION-OF-
TRAVEL

HOW DO I TAKE
A MAP BEARING?

Oh, oh. You still want to head to that mountain peak, but this time you are enshrouded in a dense fog. How are you going to get there? First, orient your map. Now, place the edge of the baseplate like a ruler with the direction-of-travel arrow pointing from your current location on the map toward your intended destination. The edge of the baseplate should exactly connect your current location and your intended destination. Being careful not to move either the map or the compass, rotate the compass housing until the north end of the compass needle centers itself exactly inside the orienting arrow. Your degree bearing is indicated at the index point. Now, without moving the compass housing, stand up holding the compass level at your waist and rotate your body until the north end of the compass needle centers itself exactly inside the orienting arrow. Your course is indicated by the direction-of-travel arrow (Figure 4–10). Follow the navigation directions indicated in taking a field bearing.

Figure 4–10 **Map Bearing.** Orient map. Place edge of compass connecting current location with destination. Make sure direction-of-travel arrow is pointing towards your destination. Rotate housing to "box" magnetic needle with orienting arrow. Read bearing at index line. Hold compass level and rotate body until needle is boxed with orienting arrow.

IT'S ON THE MAP; HOW DO I FIND IT IN THE FIELD?

You can see where you are on the map, that much is certain. You've even picked out an interesting summit on the map, not too far from where you are now, and you want to explore it. But, in scanning the terrain you're having a hard time picking the summit out of the several others clustered nearby. What do you do? Follow the directions for taking a map bearing. Once you have the established bearing and have rotated your body, holding the compass at waist level until the magnetic needle is boxed or centered within the orienting arrow, you should be able to determine which summit you want—it's the one the direction of travel arrow is pointing towards (Figure 4–11).

Figure 4–11 **Find it in the Field.** Orient map. Place edge of compass connecting current location with destination. Make sure direction-of-travel arrow is pointing towards your destination. Rotate housing to "box" magnetic needle with orienting arrow. Read bearing at index line. Hold compass level and rotate body until needle is boxed with orienting arrow. Direction-of-travel arrow is pointing at landmark.

IT'S IN THE FIELD; HOW DO I FIND IT ON THE MAP?

You can see that distant summit, and you know where you are on the map, but you have no idea which summit on the map is the one you are looking at in the field. What's a navigator to do? First, orient your map. Then, hold your compass level at waist height and point the

direction-of-travel arrow at the mountain's summit. Rotate the compass housing until the red end of the magnetic compass needle is centered (boxed) within the orienting arrow. Your bearing may be read in degrees at the center index point— where the compass housing meets the direction-of-travel arrow on the compass baseplate. Taking care not to move the map, place one edge of the compass's baseplate directly on your current location on the map. Now, without moving the compass housing or moving the map in any way, pivot the compass around your known location point until the red end of the magnetic compass needle is centered (boxed) within the orienting arrow. Draw a line, either in pencil or make it an imaginary one, along the edge of the baseplate toward the summits indicated on the map. The summit you are looking at in the field will be the one intersected by the line drawn from your location (Figure 4–12).

Figure 4–12 **Find it on the Map.** Orient map. Hold compass level and sight to landmark. Rotate compass housing and "box" magnetic needle with orienting arrow. Place compass edge on present location. Rotate compass while leaving edge on present location until needle is boxed with orienting arrow. Draw line from landmark.

ESTABLISHING BEARINGS WITHOUT ORIENTING THE MAP

Do you always have to orient a map to establish a bearing? No, although keep in mind that any time you do not orient the map, you are increasing the opportunity for error. Still, these techniques are especially useful when trying to establish a bearing on the fly and you don't need to take the time to orient the map. What I most like about learning this technique is that you can accurately plan your entire trip at home, establishing correct bearings and then writing those bearings down to use when you actually head out into the field. These "no map orientation needed" procedures are outlined in this section (Figure 4–13):

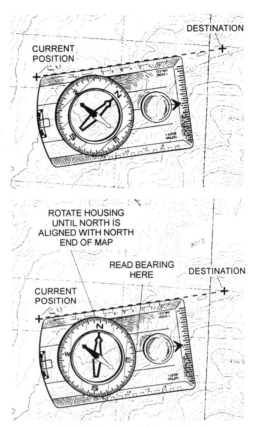

Figure 4–13 **Map Bearing without Orienting Map.** Place edge of compass connecting current location with destination. Make sure direction-of-travel arrow is pointing towards your destination. Rotate housing until the north end of azimuth ring is pointing towards the north end of the map. Read bearing at index line.

For a Map with Magnetic Lines Projected across It

If you have magnetic lines drawn on your map do not use your compass' built-in declination adjustment.

- To establish a bearing from the map (map to field)

    Connect your location with your destination, using the edge of your compass' baseplate with the direction-of-travel arrow pointing towards your destination. Being careful not to move the compass, rotate the compass housing until the orienting arrow points to magnetic north (if you don't do this correctly and end up point the orienting arrow towards the south, your bearing will be 180 degrees off) and the compass housing's orienting lines parallel the map's magnetic-north lines. Ignore the magnetic needle entirely. Your bearing may be read at the index point (Figure 4–14).

- To plot a bearing on the map (field to map)

After establishing your field bearing, do not move the dial. Place one edge of the compass on your known point on the map (with location known, place the bottom corner of the baseplate on your location with the direction-of-travel arrow pointing away; with landmark known, but location unverified, place the top corner of the baseplate on the landmark, direction-of-travel arrow pointing at the landmark). Rotate the entire compass around the point until you align the orienting lines with the magnetic lines projected on your map. Draw a line on the map along the edge of the baseplate from your known point out and that is your bearing, plotted on the map (Figure 4–15).

For a Map with No Magnetic Lines, Relying on the Border

If you do not have magnetic lines drawn on your map, you will utilize the printed edge of the map or the grid lines projected across your map. If your map does not have grid lines on it, you will need to either extend a straight line from your location, through your destination and to either the right or left printed edge of the map or draw lines on the map that parallel the printed edge of the map. You will also need to compensate for declination, which is most easily accomplished by using a compass with a built-in declination adjustment.

- To establish a bearing from the map (map to field)

Draw a straight line on the map that connects your location with your destination and extends through either the right (east) or left (west) edge of the map. Place the edge of your compass's baseplate with the direction-of-travel arrow positioned so that it is pointing in the same direction as your direction of travel would be on the map, from location to destination. Being careful not to move the compass, rotate the compass housing until the orienting lines are aligned with map's printed border or grid lines. Ignore the magnetic needle

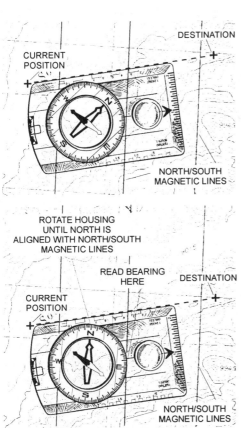

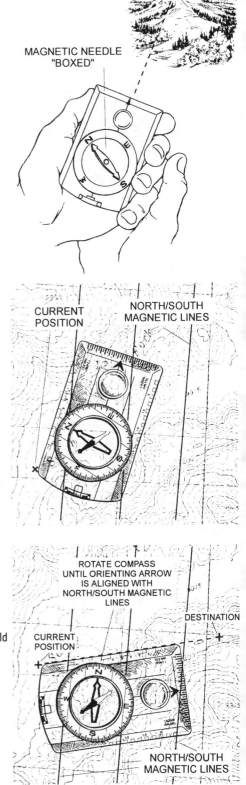

Figure 4–14 **Map Bearing with Magnetic Lines.**
Place edge of compass connecting current
location with destination. Make sure direction-of-
travel arrow is pointing towards your destination.
Rotate housing until the orienting arrow aligns
with magnetic lines. Read bearing at index line.

Figure 4–15 **Field to Map with Magnetic Lines.** Hold
compass level and sight to landmark. Rotate
compass housing and "box" magnetic needle with
orienting arrow. Place compass edge on present
location. Rotate compass while leaving edge on
present location until orienting arrow aligns with
magnetic lines. Draw line from landmark.

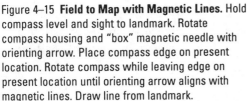

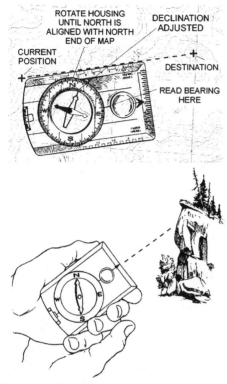

ROTATE HOUSING
UNTIL NORTH IS
ALIGNED WITH NORTH
END OF MAP

DECLINATION
ADJUSTED

CURRENT
POSITION

DESTINATION

READ BEARING
HERE

Figure 4–16 **Map to Field without Magnetic Lines.** Adjust compass for declination. Place edge of compass connecting current location with destination. Make sure direction-of-travel arrow is pointing towards your destination. Rotate housing until the orienting arrow aligns with north end of map. Read bearing at index line. Adjust declination before sighting bearing.

entirely. Your bearing may be read at the index point (Figure 4–16).

- To plot a bearing on the map (field to map)

After establishing your field bearing, do not move the dial. Place one edge of the compass on your known point on the map (with location known, place the bottom corner of the baseplate on your location with the direction-of-travel arrow pointing away; with landmark known, but location unverified, place the top corner of the baseplate on the landmark, direction-of-travel arrow pointing at the landmark). Rotate the entire compass around the point until you align the orienting lines with the printed border of the map or the grid lines on your map. Draw a line on the map along the edge of the baseplate and that is your bearing on the map (Figure 4–17).

MINIMIZING MISTAKES

I have learned over the years, and the lessons were reinforced not long ago during the Eco-Challenge, that even the most experienced navigator can make a mistake if he or she is not careful. Military cadets have been known to call in air strikes on their own platoon because of navigational errors—fortunately, this has occurred in practice sessions when personnel are afforded eternal life. Adventure racers head off in the wrong direction because fatigue inspired them to miss a critical step or misread a compass One sleep-deprived navigator in a recent Eco-Challenge was discovered holding his compass the wrong way, with the direction-of-travel arrow pointing directly at himself.

Always double-check yourself and stay ever vigilant so that you do not do the following:

- Adjust for declination in the wrong direction.

- Miscalculate the declination correction.

- Try to follow a long leg on a bearing without accounting for drift—always hike from visible point to visible point to stay on course.

- Travel with the map and compass put away because "you know where you are." Always check your position with regularity.

- Hold a compass next to a metal object, such as a belt-buckle, when trying to take a bearing.

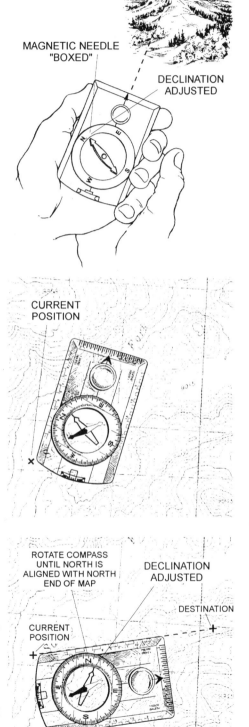

Figure 4–17 **Field to Map without Magnetic Lines.** Adjust compass for declination. Hold compass level and sight to landmark. Rotate compass housing and "box" magnetic needle with orienting arrow. Place compass edge on present location. Rotate compass while leaving edge on present location until orienting arrow aligns with north end of map.

- Take sloppy bearings. Always use the same eye and check your sighting two to three times.
- Incorrectly draw the magnetic lines on a map.
- Get confused and use the wrong end of the magnetic needle.
- Get confused and read the bearing from the opposite side of the index point.
- Point the compass's direction-of-travel arrow in the wrong direction when establishing a bearing.

Chapter Five

Practical Navigation Tips; Beyond the Basics

Now that you have learned the meat and potatoes techniques that every navigator will utilize regularly to be successful in finding his or her way, it is time to move on to the more advanced skills.

BASELINES

In the field, baselines will come into play on a regular basis as you seek to find your way. A baseline is a long line that can easily be identified and used as a point of reference on a map. A river, trail, fenceline, powerline, railway, road, river, or even a long and easily identifiable ridge can serve as a baseline (Figure 5–1). When two identifiable baselines intersect, that provides an indisputable reference point on the map. Even if you have never stepped onto a trail, I'll bet you have used baselines in giving directions to your home or a meeting place in the city. "Stay on First Street (one baseline) until you hit Meridian (another baseline) and turn left. Follow Meridian to Broadway (yet another baseline) and turn right. Drive one mile and my house is on the right." The practice remains the same in the field. "Hike two miles on the Tuolomne Trail from Bear Lake Campground until you arrive at the Twin Summits Trail. Turn right and hike until Twin Summits crosses Sparkling Creek. Our campground will be in the meadow just north of

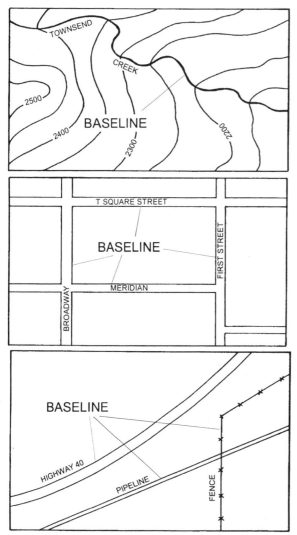

Figure 5–1

the crossing on the left side of the trail."

Skiers, hikers, and hunters frequently use baselines when heading out in the woods to explore, especially when leaving a camp or a vehicle next to a road or trail. The beauty of a good baseline is that you don't really have to keep detailed tabs on your particular course. If your camp is sitting next to a river that runs generally east/west, you could head off to the south or north, explore for a while, reverse your direction, and be assured that you will once again arrive at the baseline—in this case, the river. No real navigational headaches here. There is, however, one minor question: Once you get to the baseline (the river), should you head north or south to get back to camp? This may seem like a tough question to answer if you haven't been paying close attention to your wanderings. But, fortunately, there are several easy ways to solve this dilemma without having to resort to the time- and energy-sapping method of trial and error.

FIXING YOUR POSITION ON A BASELINE

So, you've arrived back at the river and have no idea which way to turn? No problem. First, orient your map. Then, standing next to the

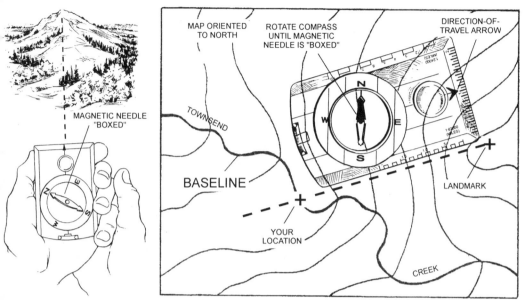

Figure 5–2 **Finding Yourself with a Baseline.** Orient map. Hold compass level and sight to a landmark. Rotate compass housing and "box" magnetic needle with orienting arrow. Place compass edge on landmark sighted. Rotate compass while leaving edge on landmark until needle is boxed with orienting arrow. Draw line from landmark. Location is where baseline and bearing intersect.

baseline (the river), take a bearing on a distant and recognizable landmark. To do this, hold your compass level at waist height and point the direction-of-travel arrow at the landmark. Rotate the compass housing until the red end of the magnetic compass needle is centered (boxed) within the orienting arrow. Your bearing may be read in degrees at the center index point—where the compass housing meets the direction-of-travel arrow on the compass baseplate. Taking care not to move the map, place one edge of the compass's baseplate directly on the landmark, with the direction-of-travel arrow pointing from the baseline (river) towards the landmark. Now, without moving the compass housing or moving the map in any way, pivot the compass around the landmark point until the red end of the magnetic compass needle is centered (boxed) within the orienting arrow. Draw a line, either in pencil or make it an imaginary one, along the edge of the baseplate until it intersects with the baseline (river) you are standing beside. Your location on the river is where the two lines intersect. Now, assuming you know where your camp is on the river, you should know whether to head east or west to return to your shelter (Figure 5–2).

Figure 5–3

AIMING OFF

Another way to find your camp along the river is to intentionally miss the camp so far to the north or south that you will know which way to head. In other words, make your mistake so bad that it becomes an intentional error you can correct once you arrive at the river. For instance, you wandered well away from camp in a generally northern direction and want to head back. You are somewhat sure where the camp lies by looking at a saddle in a distant ridge behind you and realizing that your camp is somewhere below that. The problem is, if you head toward the saddle and arrive at the river, will you arrive just east or just west of the camp? You have no way of knowing. The solution: Pick a route that will position you well east of the saddle. That way, once you arrive at the baseline (river), you know for certain that camp lies to the west. Now all you do is hike along the river until you reach camp. Simple!

BRACKETING

This technique, frequently used by hunters, wildlife watchers, and fishers, involves a little more detailed analysis of your location along a baseline. This method, called "bracketing," is especially useful when you leave a vehicle parked alongside a remote Forest Service road. A bracket is nothing more than an identifiable boundary that lets you know you should turn around and head the other way on a baseline to get to your destination. A bracket is also useful in helping you determine if the baseline you are on is actually the baseline you want; this is extremely valuable when wandering the mountains of the West where forests are crisscrossed with Forest Service roads that look decidedly similar.

I utilize brackets frequently when leaving my vehicle beside a remote road to go backcountry skiing. On the drive in, I'll identify one landmark that I know is about one-half mile from where I want to park and then another one within a quarter mile and one more within a few hundred yards. Most often, I will drive past my parking area to establish similar brackets in the other direction. If the road is blocked to vehicles, but still continues on, I'll head off on my skis to establish the brackets before I dare head off away from the road. Brackets can be bridges, road signs, rock falls, large boulders, deadfalls, a large and recognizable tree, etc. Forget trying to remember the brackets. Instead, record them meticulously on a sheet of paper. Once I return to the road from my skiing, I'll use the brackets to tell me which way to turn to get back to my vehicle.

MAKING A BEARING A BASELINE

You are camping in the desert and there are no rivers, fencelines, roads, trails, or anything else that you can see fit to use as a physical baseline. Nevertheless, you want to go off exploring and would like to be reasonably sure you could return to camp without difficulty. What do you do? When there isn't a baseline to be had, make your own. No, I don't mean begin construction of a fence or trail. This baseline will be imaginary.

To do this, take a bearing off a prominent landmark while standing in your camp by holding your compass level at waist height and pointing the direction-of-travel arrow at the landmark. Rotate the compass housing until the red end of the magnetic compass needle is centered (boxed) within the orienting arrow. Your bearing may be read in degrees at the center index point—where the compass housing meets the direction-of-travel arrow on the compass baseplate. Write this bearing down. That bearing and the line-of-sight you just took have become your baseline (Figure 5–4).

So, off you go, merrily exploring the desert terrain. The time comes to return to camp. Set your compass so that your baseline

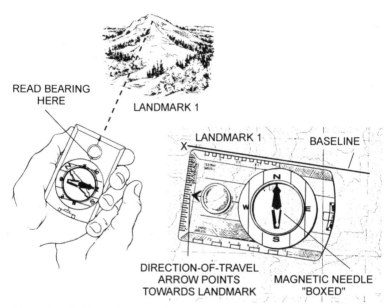

READ BEARING
HERE

LANDMARK 1

LANDMARK 1   BASELINE

DIRECTION-OF-TRAVEL
ARROW POINTS
TOWARDS LANDMARK

MAGNETIC NEEDLE
"BOXED"

Figure 5–4 **Making a Baseline.** Orient map. Hold compass level and sight to landmark. Rotate compass housing and "box" magnetic needle with orienting arrow. Place compass edge on landmark sighted. Rotate compass while leaving edge on landmark until needle is boxed with orienting arrow. Draw line from landmark. This is your made baseline.

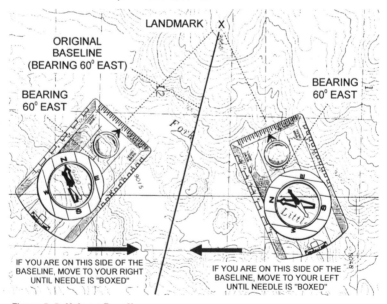

LANDMARK

ORIGINAL
BASELINE
(BEARING 60° EAST)

BEARING
60° EAST

BEARING
60° EAST

IF YOU ARE ON THIS SIDE OF THE
BASELINE, MOVE TO YOUR RIGHT
UNTIL NEEDLE IS "BOXED"

IF YOU ARE ON THIS SIDE OF THE
BASELINE, MOVE TO YOUR LEFT
UNTIL NEEDLE IS "BOXED"

Figure 5–5 **Using a Baseline.**

bearing is at the index point. Point the direction-of-travel arrow at the landmark you sighted off earlier that day and begin walking to the right or left until you have once again centered the magnetic compass needle within the orienting arrow. You are now back on the baseline. Of course, the question now arises, which way do you turn on the baseline. Well, if you were smart, you aimed off as described above, ending up on the baseline closer to the landmark so that you know you will have to follow a back bearing from the landmark to return to camp along the baseline bearing (Figure 5–5).

You can eliminate the worry of having to aim off by adding a second baseline to the mix. Before you leave camp, establish a bearing towards a second easily recognizable landmark and write that bearing down. What you are banking on here is the fact that two straight lines can only intersect in one place (Mr. Frumplemeyer's ninth grade geometry class covered this if you had been paying attention). This comes into play once you have arrived back at your first baseline. If you have a map and know where the camp is on the map, you can quickly determine which way you should head. First, orient the map. Next, draw the first baseline on the map so that it becomes visible, not imaginary. Now, hold your compass level at waist height and point the direction-of-travel arrow at the second landmark. Rotate the compass housing until the red end of the magnetic compass needle is centered (boxed) within the orienting arrow. Your bearing may be read in degrees at the center index point—where the compass housing meets the direction-of-travel arrow on the compass baseplate. Taking care not to move the map, place one edge of the compass's baseplate directly on the second landmark, with the direction-of-travel arrow pointing from the baseline towards the landmark. Now, without moving the compass housing or moving the map in any way, pivot the compass around the landmark point until the red end of the magnetic compass needle is centered (boxed) within the orienting arrow. Draw a line, either in pencil or make it an imaginary one, along the edge of the baseplate until it intersects with the baseline you are standing next to. Your location on the baseline is where the two lines intersect. You should now know which way to turn to get back to your camp (Figure 5–6).

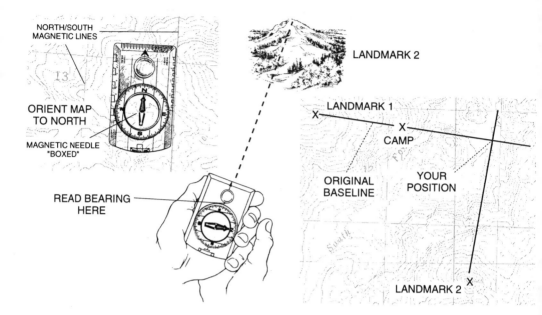

Figure 5–6 **Using Two Made Baselines.** Orient map. Hold compass level and sight to landmark. Rotate compass housing and "box" magnetic needle with orienting arrow. Place compass edge on landmark sighted. Rotate compass while leaving edge on landmark until needle is boxed with oriented arrow. Draw line from landmark. Repeat for second baseline.

What if you don't have a map? Hold your compass level at waist height and point the direction-of-travel arrow at your second landmark. Rotate the compass housing until the red end of the magnetic compass needle is centered (boxed) within the orienting arrow. Read the bearing. Compare it to the bearing you wrote down when you sighted off this landmark from camp. Now move to the right or the left on your baseline and take another bearing off the second landmark. Compare it again to the bearing you wrote down. The closer your bearing is to the bearing you wrote down, the closer you are to camp, which means that is the direction you should head.

PINPOINTING YOUR POSITION; TRIANGULATION

It is important to realize that even with the best navigator and the best hand-held compass, error still manages to creep into the mix. On average, each bearing may be off anywhere from one to four degrees, depending on numerous factors influencing the outcome. This means

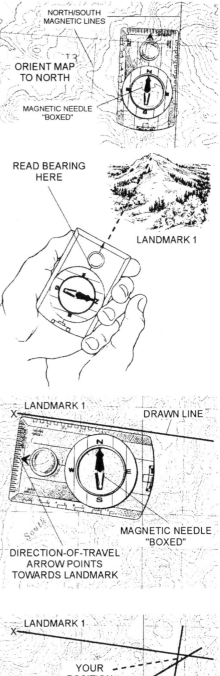

that if you really want to establish an exact, or as close to exact location as you're going to get, you'll need to establish not one, not two, but three baselines. Where those three baselines intersect will be your location on the map. Establishing your absolute position fix using triangulation will be much more effective if you can select landmarks that are relatively near to you and as spread out as possible around the points of the compass.

First, orient the map. Then, hold your compass level at waist height and point the direction-of-travel arrow at the first landmark. Rotate the compass housing until the red end of the magnetic compass needle is centered (boxed) within the orienting arrow. Your bearing may be read in degrees at the center index point—where the compass housing meets the direction-of-travel arrow on the compass baseplate. Taking care not to move the map, place one edge of the compass' baseplate directly on the landmark, with the direction-of-travel arrow pointing towards the landmark. Now, without moving the compass

Figure 5–7 **Triangulation Orient map**. Hold compass level and sight to landmark. Rotate compass housing and "box" magnetic needle with orienting arrow. Place compass edge on landmark sighted. Rotate compass while leaving edge on landmark until needle is "boxed" with orienting arrow. Draw line from landmark. Repeat process. Your location is found where the lines intersect.

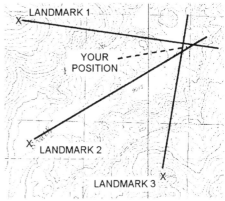

housing or moving the map in any way, pivot the compass around the landmark point until the red end of the magnetic compass needle is centered (boxed) within the orienting arrow. Draw a line in pencil along the edge of the compass's baseplate. Repeat the steps with a second and third landmark. The area or triangle bounded by all three lines will be the area in which you are located. The farther away the landmarks you sight off, the larger the triangle. The closer the landmarks, the smaller the triangle and the more accurate your fix (Figure 5–7).

DEAD RECKONING

I once thought that this meant to navigate from the hip because all of your other resources were exhausted, until I began sailing. It was then that I learned the origin of the term is based in nautical history (ancient mariners relied on this method to find their way across uncharted waters) and refers instead to reckoning by logical deduction. The word "dead" actually came from a contraction of deduction—ded. So, in reality, this is "ded.(deduction) reckoning," which makes much more sense to me.

Ded reckoning is not as accurate as other forms of navigation, but it will suffice, especially in those circumstances when the identifiable land features are few and far between. You must start with an established point of origin or a fix. Mark this point on the map. From this point, establish a compass heading and then stick to it for a measurable distance. Military personnel are taught to silently count off the number of steps they have walked and that is as good a method as any. Consider for the average human, each normal walking step is approximately 2.5 feet long. That means, if you count one for every time your right foot hits the ground, you can tally up 5 feet of distance covered. If you want to be really accurate, put a pebble in a pocket for every one hundred times your right foot hits the ground. Each pebble in your pocket will then equal about 500 feet.

Estimate your second established point on the map by counting pebbles and multiplying by five hundred. Since one mile equals 5,280 feet, you can use the map's scale to estimate how far on the map you have traveled. Mark the second point on the map. That point has been established by ded reckoning. For obvious reasons, the longer the distance you cover, the more likely a larger error will be made. If you decide to change direction at this second point, establish another compass heading and begin counting steps anew. Each time you change direction, establish another ded reckoning point on the map and in this way you can roughly chart your course and position.

Another useful application for ded reckoning doesn't involve a map at all—only your compass and an accurate measurement of time or distance. Say you have no map, but want to head out from point A to explore the surrounding terrain and still have a reasonable shot at arriving back at point A again. The terrain is featureless, so establishing a bearing as a baseline is out of the question, What do you do? From point A, head out at an established bearing, making sure to write it down so that you do not forget it. Either keep time with your watch, or measure your steps as outlined above. When it comes time to change direction, mark it down as point B. Record the elapsed time or steps counted between points A and B, establish your new bearing, and then remember to write the new bearing down.

Repeat these steps every time you change direction until you decide it is time to head back to point A again. To be precise, you must first establish a distance scale so that you can accurately, draw a map using your recorded elapsed time or distance measurements. For instance, you might establish that every fifteen minutes or 250 steps represents

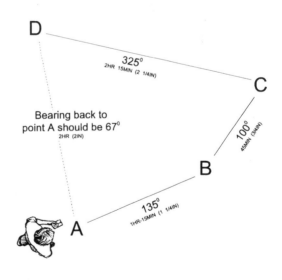

Figure 5–8 **Dead Reckoning.**

one-fourth inch. Beginning with point A either drawn on a piece of paper or scratched into the dirt, measure your elapsed distance to point B using the same bearing you followed earlier in the day. From point B, place the bearing to point C on the index line of the compass, point the direction-of-travel arrow towards point C and once again measure the correct distance covered. Repeat this until you have plotted your course on the ground or on the paper with one last leg left unplotted—the leg returning you to point A. Pointing your direction of travel arrow at point A from the last point plotted, say point L, turn the dial and center (box) the magnetic needle with the orienting arrow. Read the bearing at the index point—this is the bearing you will follow to get back to A. Keep in mind, you were using ded reckoning, so don't expect to be exact, but if you were careful, you should come very close (Figure 5–8).

ESTIMATING DISTANCE

Estimating distance is useful to paddlers, hunters, or any adventurers who may be contemplating a paddle or trek to a distance peak, island or point in the desert that appears deliciously close. Remember, my friends, things are not always as they appear. Objects will assuredly appear closer than they are if the atmosphere is brilliantly clear or if they are viewed across flat, open terrain such as sand, water, or snow. If you are carrying a range finder, you're home free. Chances are, though, that you've opted to save the expense, weight, and bulk of this item which leaves you to estimate.

One tried and true method involves winking. Ever notice that if you alternately open one eye and then the other, objects you are gazing at appear to move back and forth? Well, you can use this to your advantage, providing you know the width in miles or feet of the object from which you are estimating your distance. For paddlers, this involves finding out how wide a distant point or island is. For hunters or hikers, you'll need to know how wide a plateau or mountain is. With one eye closed, extend your arm and hold up one finger. Using the open eye, sight the finger to the opposite side of the object (left eye to right corner/right eye to left corner). Now, close that eye and open

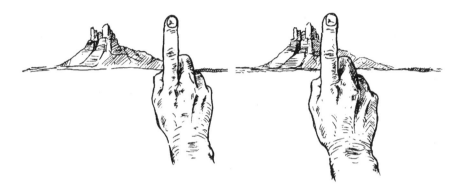

Figure 5–9

the other to look at the same finger. Estimate how far across the object your finger appeared to jump—one eighth, one quarter, one half, one? Now, divide the width of the object into the fractions represented by your finger observation. For example, if your finger appeared to jump halfway across an object you know to be one mile wide, then the movement equaled one-half mile. The formula for establishing distance is to multiply that distance by 10. That means 10 x 1/2 = 5 or, the distance you are from the object is approximately five miles (Figure 5–9).

Chapter Six

Planning Your Outing

- Timing Your Trip
- Estimating Your Traveling Speed
- Staying on Course / Finding the Trail
- Picking a Route When Your Life Depends on It

Always plan your hike and hike your plan. This advice goes for any adventure, whether a hike or not. That way, if you get into trouble, and you left an itinerary of your trip with a friend, rescuers should be able to find you easily. When I taught outdoor skills courses for Adventure 16 in Southern California, I mandated that all of my students learn to leave detailed itineraries with a family member, close friend, or responsible neighbor. For obvious reasons, it is better for you if this person has a vested interest in your safe return—either because they like you or because you owe them a lot of money. What you will leave with them is as follows: name and emergency contact numbers for everyone with whom you are traveling; your vehicle description and license number; your anticipated return time; your route and intended campsites, complete with a map with the route highlighted if possible; an alternate route should weather or something else alter your plans; and the person to contact to initiate a rescue if you are overdue. Don't forget to notify your friend when you do return so that they don't worry and, most importantly, so that a rescue doesn't get called out when you are sitting safely in front of a hot meal at home.

TIMING YOUR TRIP

Getting stuck out for the night is not, strictly speaking, the same as getting lost, but both typically occur because you've miscalculated either trip distance, or trip time, or perhaps both. Learning to accurately estimate how long a particular hike will take you is an essential part of the navigator's planning game (especially with day trips, since you'll probably not be carrying any camping gear). If you are in the habit of trying to play it thin so you arrive—you hope—back at your camp or your car the second it gets absolutely dark, expect to get burned from time to time. It is always better to plan conservatively. A simple formula applies to almost all circumstances.

Once you have decided where you want to go and when, the most important thing to determine is the time it is slated to get dark on that day. Depending on the terrain and the season, darkness can settle over you like a blanket in just five minutes (in mountainous jungle during the monsoon) or in one-half hour (as it does at the beach in the summer). Any local newspaper has sunrise and sunset information. Then, by taking note of the time you plan to begin hiking, paddling, or skiing, you can calculate the window of time you have. If you start at noon and dusk falls at six, you have six hours of daylight.

When estimating how much time a trek will take, keep in mind that, for the majority of outings, you are going to have far more energy at the beginning of the outing and far less in reserve towards the end. That means that if you start at noon and it gets dark at six, it's best not to wait till three o'clock to charge down the trail more rapidly, hoping to get all the way to your destination and back to the car that day—in the daylight. Better to turn around at two or two-thirty, and allow for a slower pace. Time estimates can get iffy, for instance, when the hike out is virtually all uphill. While you might figure that going downhill will be much faster, the pounding your knees and ankles will take, coupled with your increased fatigue, can sap the life out of even the most sturdy limbs. I always estimate that it will take me one-and-a-half times longer to return from a destination than it did to get to it, and I plan accordingly.

Of course, not all trips proceed according to plan, and that is the beauty of adventuring. What this means, however, is that there will be times when it is probably prudent to turn around before reaching your

destination—unless you want
to hike in the dark. Knowing
when to turn around involves
knowing not so much what
time it is, although that is
useful too, but how much
sunlight is left in the day.
Although you may have
planned well, perhaps you
overlooked the fact that the
last two miles of the hike
back will be along the bottom
of the canyon and that day's
light will be chased away
from the canyon's depths

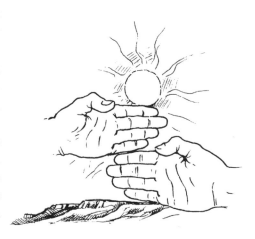

Figure 6–1

long before the sun actually sets. So, how do you estimate when the
sun will disappear behind a ridge and twilight will settle in? By using
your eyes and hands. While I realize that not all hands are the same
size, this trick serves to roughly estimate time no matter how large
your digits are. Look towards the sun, though not directly at it, and
hold your hand an arm's length away. Line up the bottom of your
pinkie (your fourth finger) with the top of the visible horizon (the top
of the canyon wall or a distant ridge, for example). Every four fingers
up from the horizon towards the sun account for approximately one
hour. So, if you hold both your hands out, with one hand on top of the
other and the sun is sitting just above the index finger of your top
hand, you can be fairly sure that you have two hours of sunlight left in
the day (Figure 6–1).

ESTIMATING YOUR TRAVELING SPEED

Hitting the Trail at the Speed of . . . Well . . . a Slow Moving Rock Perhaps?

Estimating your rate of travel is essential when determining the amount
of time it will require to traverse a particular route. It's no fun planning
a three day hike and then finding you are only halfway home, out of
fuel, and out of food on the third day. In general, travel times should be
estimated as follows, although keep in mind that you or someone in

your group may hike a little faster or even slower. Always hike at the comfort pace of the slowest member of your group:

- Hiking in boots on level ground with a light load and moderate elevation gain - 3 to 4 mph.
- Hiking in boots at 6,000 feet of elevation or higher with some hills - 3 to 4 mph.
- Hiking in boots bushwhacking or traveling cross country without the benefit of trails - 1.5 to 2 mph.
- Hiking in boots steep climbing up ridges and mountain sides - .5 to 1 mph.
- Hiking in snowshoes on open terrain with gentle ups and downs - 2 to 3 mph.
- Trail running on level ground with a light load and moderate elevation gain - 6 to 8 mph.
- Trail running at 6,000 feet of elevation or higher with moderate elevation gain and loss - 5 to 7 mph.

According to the U.S. Army, the following way is a good method to gauge hiking speed. If you are female and walk between 20 to 21 steps every 10 seconds, or are male and walk between 16 to 17 steps every 10 seconds, you are traveling at approximately 3 miles per hour. Stepping out at 27 to 28 steps every 10 seconds as a female or 20 to 21 steps every 10 seconds as a male means you are blazing down the trail at approximately 4 miles per hour. Of course, knowing your estimated speed is one thing; using it to determine how long it will take you to get from point A to B is yet another. For that, you have to factor in elevation gain and loss. Although conservative, most experts suggest adding one hour of time for every 1,000 feet of elevation gain. So, to estimate how long your hike is going to take, determine your hike length, elevation gain, and estimated speed of travel. Assuming you hike at 4 miles per hour, a 4 mile hike with 2,000 feet of elevation gain might take you as long as three hours.

STAYING ON COURSE / FINDING THE TRAIL

How do you know if you are on the right trail or not? Trails are marked in many different ways throughout the country. Blazes, a diamond, or a dotted "I" carved into a tree about six to eight feet off of the ground are common. So are painted blazes or metal plates nailed to a tree. These identifiable trail markers are placed on both sides of the tree and at regular intervals so that you will be able to spot the next blaze within a few feet of leaving the last one. Following blazes comes with a caveat however—trees fall or get burned. Sometimes, unthinking backwoods travelers carve their own blazes to help them find their way back to the original route, confusing the matter. You have to use your head and keep a sharp eye out. On occasion, finding the next blaze involves a little sleuthing. Don't panic and, above all, don't just head out blindly along a treadway just because it "looks like a trail." Remember that animals walk in the woods too, and the trails they leave often resemble human footpaths.

When the track heads above the treeline or through open and treeless areas like deserts or vast plains, trails often are marked with "ducks" or cairns—piles of rocks. Sometimes, in challenging terrain where route finding is a matter of life and death, cairns have been replaced by five-foot high wands with reflective tape or paint. The Mount Washington area in New Hampshire and Mount Katahdin in Maine are two such areas.

PICKING A ROUTE WHEN YOUR LIFE DEPENDS ON IT

Navigational Challenges in Various Terrain

Jungle   Thinking of attempting to track a straight line? Hah! Forget it. The jungle and many rainforests are so dense that you will have to make use of wildlife paths, ridge lines, streams, dry river beds, or established human trails. You will find that all of the above will have one thing in common—they thread their way through the dense understory by running along the bottom or parallel to the valley floors. This is fine as long as your intended route of travel is going the same way, but more often than not, it isn't. In the jungle perhaps more than anywhere else, it is essential that you are skilled in the use of the compass so that you can snake your way around obstacles, along valleys, and over low ridges while still maintaining a semblance of staying on your intended course. Landmarks, if you can see them, will become extremely valuable. Travel during the day and get off any established path at night; animals—frequently predators—will cruise along these same trails. If you select a trail, try to pick one that is heading up and out of the valley floor as opposed to meandering along it. Trails that follow valley floors are often overgrown, will more likely involve trickier stream crossings, and will generally be muckier. If you are really in doubt about which way to head, the tried and true recommendation of following the nearest water course downstream is a good one. Eventually, waterways will lead to human habitation, although be prepared to follow a meandering course that might take you twice as long to cover the same ground you would have covered had you attempted a more direct course of navigational route-finding.

Desert   Although maps of the desert regions in the United States are fairly accurate, such is not the case internationally. In order to get to a location where you have a hope of finding human life and preserving your own, it is essential that you know, with reasonable certainty, where you are now so that it is possible to make an educated guess and determine your direction of travel. If you have no idea where you are now, a map becomes useless, and heading off in any direction is, at best, a roll of the dice. If you are in a survival situation because of a broken down vehicle, and you have no idea where you are, it might be best to stay put. Officials who provide information to those traveling into the Australian Outback mandate that you never leave your vehicle since it is far easier for a rescue team to find the vehicle than a person on the move. Should you decide that moving is in your best interests, then travel only in the early morning or late evening, when the sun will not sap the very life from your limbs. Leave positive instructions with your vehicle indicating your direction of travel. If animal trails exist and they are heading in your desired direction of travel, use them. Avoid the temptation to follow watercourses or dry stream beds unless their direction matches the heading you need to follow. Many watercourses in the desert meander only to depressions or dry lakes inland. However, if the watercourse you come across is full of water, and you are in the desert, you should strongly consider staying put—water is life! Pick your way around dunes as this will conserve valuable energy; the walking is typically easier and the footing firmer in the valleys between dunes. Keep checking and double-checking your heading to be sure you are on course. And, whenever possible, use distant landmarks to keep your travels from drifting right or left of your intended destination.

Arctic   This is the one time you need to forget the advice to hike downstream to find your way to human habitation. A waterway flowing in a northerly direction will likely lead you away from humans, not towards them. In the winter, valley floors are often the easiest places to navigate since they are somewhat sheltered from the wind that sweeps across the ridges, and the snow has most likely covered any areas choked by underbrush. Always question your compass—being so close to the magnetic pole can mess with a compass's accuracy—and back up your navigational decisions and headings with celestial observation and a sundial or watch (as described in Chapter Four) or a GPS. Navigating over vast areas of smooth and often featureless snow can also be exhausting and disorienting.

Coastline   It certainly won't be a straight course, but your route will be an unmistakable one if you choose to follow a coastline. Be aware that any coastal travel will likely involve sweeping winds with driving sand, loose rocks, slippery shores, shifting sands, impassable cliffs, and swampy terrain at river mouths. For those times when you have to head inland to negotiate an impassable feature, be sure to take careful and accurate bearings so that you will not waste valuable time and energy beating around the underbrush trying to find your way back to the coast and the path leading down to the beach on the other side of the cliff or swamp.

Snow   Route finding can become a nightmare in the winter if you get off course and are not paying close attention to landmarks. This is because many of the usual baselines such as trails, fencelines, and fire roads are buried under a deep blanket of snow. Trail blazes, too, will often be buried. In addition, estimating height and distance gets harder since contours are rounded off and depressions are filled in. Keeping dry can be a challenge since marshes, lakes, and even small streams are covered by snow and ice, but often not deeply enough to hold your weight. What appears to be the quickest route, may not be the safest. Always err on the side of caution and work your way around suspect areas. It is essential that you travel with your map and compass always handy. Make fastidious note of each and every recognizable landmark and your position in relationship to it, and find that point on the map, too. Avoid steep slopes that could spell avalanche danger. Keep in mind that, if your route takes you across streams or rivers, the safest time to cross them via a snow bridge will be in the early morning hours when they are most likely to be frozen solidly. Watch out for warming trends which can spell disaster. That stream you are planning to cross could turn into a raging flood in only a short time if a warming trend and rain triggers snowmelt.

Chapter Seven

Specialized Navigational Aids

ALTIMETERS

Can altimeters be used as navigation tools?

You bet! Altimeters are very useful additions to your navigational system. They're also a worthwhile tool to help forecast weather changes and estimate elevation loss and gain. Pocket altimeters measure and then convert barometric pressure into altitude readings, even if it is dark or you are completely fogged in. By constantly registering present elevation, an altimeter can be useful in determining when you have reached a given elevation and, consequently, a contour line on a topographic map. That information can then be used to guide you along that contour line or elevation to your eventual destination—minimizing energy-wasting searches for the "Camp I know is here somewhere!"

The best altimeters compensate temperature so that temperature fluctuations will not affect the reading too much. To be really useful, however, an altimeter must have measurable increments of no more than 50 feet and must be accurate to within 100 feet. If you think that you'll be rough on your altimeter, then an electronic one will best suit your needs; it also will be easier to read and use. For greatest accuracy, a mechanical altimeter with geared movement is the best choice. Mechanical altimeters have one distinct advantage over electronic ones; they have no batteries to fail, making them the best choice for extended cold-weather use.

One last word of advice. Since the altimeter registers barometric changes, it will "adjust" altitude readings as the barometric pressure rises and falls, even though the altimeter may remain at a constant altitude. You will be wise to learn to recalibrate the altimeter on a regular basis using known points of elevation as you pass over them—in fact, your altimeter will quickly become useless weight unless you regularly recalibrate it.

USING THE ALTIMETER, PRACTICALLY SPEAKING

Figure 7–1

Remember in the earlier chapters when I spoke of baselines? Well, if you are on a baseline, or come across a baseline during your travels, you can use the baseline and your altimeter to confirm your position. For example, the visibility is dropping as you proceed up the ridge toward camp, just below the summit. You can no longer sight off the summit and are becoming unsure of your location on the mountain. You are, however, hiking next to a stream and you can pinpoint its location on the map. That stream is a baseline. If you think about it, each contour line as you proceed up the mountain is also a baseline, since as the stream flows downhill, it intersects with each contour only once. You whip out your altimeter, knowing you recently calibrated it to a known elevation and read your altitude—9,260 feet. Your finger traces a line up the creek to elevation 9,260 feet and, presto, there you are (Figure 7–1).

GLOBAL POSITIONING SYSTEMS

The Global Positioning System (GPS) is made up of a network of twenty-four satellites that orbit the earth twice a day transmitting precise time and position information. With a hand-held GPS receiver, you can determine your location anywhere on earth (Figure 7–2).

A GPS receiver works by listening to the signals of three or more satellites. By measuring the time interval between the transmission and the reception of a satellite signal, the receiver calculates distance between the user and the satellite.

Figure 7–2

Using the distance measurements of at least three satellites and some fancy math footwork known as algorithms, the GPS establishes an accurate position fix. Three satellites must be acquired for the GPS to accurately display longitude and latitude, and four satellites must be acquired to add elevation to the mix. Keep in mind, that since the U.S. Department of Defense controls the signals going out to civilian receivers and intentionally varies the signal in a process called Selective Availability, the horizontal accuracy of a GPS will vary from 40 feet (15 meters) to 327 feet (100 meters). Altitude or vertical accuracy is less, varying between 327 feet (100 meters) and 510 feet (156 meters). This means you should not plan on using your GPS as an altimeter.

WHY WOULD I WANT A GPS?

A GPS is an ideal tool for those times when you are adventuring in relatively featureless areas such as the desert or vast snowfields or when visibility is reduced to almost nil because of overcast and fog. With a GPS, you can determine your exact location on a map with a simple press of a button, you can enter a location from a map into memory and the GPS will help guide you there, or you can store information in the GPS as you travel so that it will help to guide you back.

In my opinion, being able to turn to a GPS to establish your exact position, no matter what the weather, is perhaps its most valuable feature. However, GPS's are a long way from being the magical wand you wave to always get home safely. High mountains, deep canyons, dense forests, and jungle canopy—all will obscure the signals a GPS relies on, making the unit useless.

What about gauging your speed? True, manuals and advertisements and even the odd review or two have touted the GPS as a tool that can measure your speed, estimate your time of travel, and continuously plot your route so that you can observe your progress on the screen and make corrections as needed. The problem with this claim, however, is that these features will work only as long as you leave the GPS in the "on" position, draining the batteries, and hold the GPS either in front of you or mount the antennae to the top of your pack while the GPS rides in a pack pocket—far from practical. At this point in time, I would recommend that if you purchase a GPS, buy it on its route-finding and positioning merits alone.

There is also a hidden danger in the power of the GPS, one that can lull you into a false sense of security. Even with a GPS, you would be foolhardy to venture far afield without being skilled in map and compass navigation techniques. What if the batteries die, or you drop the receiver or the antennae is broken or it drowned in a lake? Without a GPS, could you determine where you are and how to head for home using just a map and compass? If your answer is anything less than a firm and emphatic "ABSOLUTELY NO PROBLEM!" you might want to reevaluate your approach and brush up on your navigational skills by rereading this book for starters.

WHAT FEATURES DO I NEED IN A GPS?

Most GPS receivers will allow you to display information in longitude and latitude, Universal Transverse Mercator (UTM grids that many Bureau of Land Management and other survey maps utilize), or military grid. Some, such as the Trimble, display actual map quadrant names and then give inch measurements to aid in position location on the listed map. As a minimum, your GPS should support both UTM and longitude / latitude grids, because with those two grids, you'll be able to utilize the GPS anywhere in the world.

Route and Go To functions are essential. The Route function allows you to program up to ten waypoints (some GPS's allow even more) and will then automatically switch from waypoint to waypoint as you hike along your route—without you even having to touch a button. The Go To function also will guide you, but it is a single application only, meaning that you have to enter the next waypoint into the system manually each time.

Steering is perhaps the second most useful tool your GPS offers—if you are willing to hike with your GPS on all the time, because a GPS cannot calculate direction if you are standing still. While a compass simply points you in the direction you need to go, a GPS in Go To or Route mode will not only direct you towards your next waypoint, it can tell you how far you have traveled, how far you have to go, if you have wandered off course and how to get back, and when you have reached your destination.

Personally, I use my GPS to establish a bearing, which it easily does when in either the Route or Go To function. A simple press of a button and my bearing to the next waypoint will be displayed. It is a simple matter for me to then turn off my GPS or place it in battery save mode if I'm planning to use it again soon, whip out my compass, set the bearing, center (box) the orienting arrow and hike off in the direction my direction-of-travel arrow points. I must admit that I also really enjoy using the distance function so that I can estimate how much farther I have to go—as the crow flies of course.

The more pricey a GPS becomes, the more features it offers—up to complete personal computer interface for uploading and downloading navigational information.

WILL USING A GPS GUARANTEE I'LL NEVER GET LOST?

Yeah, right, and I'll soon be the King of Siam. The GPS is only a tool and is subject to the user making proper use of it to ensure navigational accuracy. Every coordinate must be entered correctly and then every coordinate must be read correctly. It's a mass of numbers and letters that to the untrained eye can appear confusing and even to the trained eye under stress can seem mystifying. During the 1996 ESPN Extreme Games Adventure Race, each team used a hand-held GPS to stay on course over the 360 miles of dense wilderness and swamp, and I had a hoot watching them veer off course time and again. Would it have been easier with a map and compass? Heck no! But the GPS was no guarantee of success either. The bottom line: the teams that did well were the ones that had the most experience using the tools at their disposal. Want to stay found? Then practice, practice, practice.

PUTTING YOUR GPS TO USE

Before you use your GPS, you must set it to the local time. Next, determine whether you want it to read in feet, meters, or miles for distance measurement and select the coordinate system you want to use, such as latitude and longitude or UTM. Finally, you'll need to initialize your GPS by either turning it on and letting it establish its own coordinate fix (this can take up to fifteen minutes from a cold start) or by entering in the UTM or latitude and longitude coordinates for your location, if you know them. Once your GPS has established your current coordinate fix, save it by giving this fix a name and number (for example, Trlhd 1). Now, plot your course by entering the coordinates along your route and give each waypoint a name and a number (I prefer to number sequentially).

As you are moving along, your GPS will give you a current position fix every time you turn it on. From this position fix, you can use the GPS to determine a bearing towards and an "as the crow flies" distance to your next waypoint or final destination. Here is where your compass and map skills come in. While the information your GPS is giving you is very valuable, it is almost useless without also turning to your basic navigation tools. Once the GPS has given you a bearing, you'll need to turn to your compass to orient yourself to follow that bearing. True, you can use a GPS for this direction finding as long as you leave it on and are in Go To mode, but it takes much longer. Also, while the GPS has given you a bearing to follow and also provided distance information in a straight line, it can tell you nothing about the lay of the land. It could be pointing you right at a cliff for all you know. A quick glance at your map with the bearing information in hand will tell you all you need to know about how easy or difficult the terrain ahead is. Then, using your compass and map together, you can plot a safe and easy route to get you where you need to be.

MAKING SENSE OF GPS SPEAK

Thanks to the introduction of GPS into our navigational world, you will encounter a new lingo, or an adaptation of standard lingo in manuals and instruction books. The following will hopefully help you to slice through a bit of the confusion.

- Azimuth - another word for bearing.

- Coordinate - GPS relies on coordinates, which are nothing more than a series of numbers that indicate the map and the grid where the position displayed is located. Latitude and longitude and UTM eastings and northings are nothing more than coordinates on a grid.

- Differential GPS - If your GPS is a differential GPS it relies on a method of compensating for Selective Availability to improve the accuracy of the GPS to within 16.4 feet or 5 meters.

- Grid - A grid is a pattern of squares on your map which serve to fix your position. Coordinates will provide numbers that allow you to find a horizontal line and also a vertical line and follow them to the point of intersection, placing you within that particular grid.

- Latitude and longitude - Latitude lines (horizontal) run parallel to the equator, and longitude lines (vertical) are drawn to connect each pole. Coordinates are measured in degrees, minutes, and seconds.

- Map Datum - A datum refers to the reference point from which all maps are drawn. GPS is based universally on a grid for the entire earth that a GPS can interpret anywhere in the world called WGS-84. Unfortunately, many maps were published before GPS so they utilize different datums—reference points. In North America, the datum is called the North American Datum 1927 or NAD27. Be sure your GPS can interpret the map datums for the areas you will be in.

- RS-232 - This is the standard type of connection to your computer and refers to the serial port that will allow your GPS to communicate with your personal computer.

- TFF (Time To First Fix) - This is the amount of time it will take your GPS receiver to make its first position fix after it has been in the off position for over a month, has lost its memory, or has been moved for over three hundred miles without an interim fix. Typically, this won't amount to more than fifteen minutes.

- Waypoint - A waypoint refers to the coordinates of a location that you will have to enter or read on the GPS. Waypoints are stored in your GPS's memory and may be recalled with the push of a button.

Prologue

A Peek into the Future

There is little doubt that the influences of the electronic age and the concurrent and rapid developments of hand-held, land-use GPS (Global Positioning Systems) receivers are being felt throughout the wilderness navigation world. As GPS prices bottom out around the $150 to $250 range, they are becoming very attractive to more than just the tech-weenie-gotta-have-the-latest-gadget crowd or the rescue personnel and professional users where the majority of limited sales have predominantly been.

Map companies such as DeLorme, Trails Illustrated, Tom Harrison, and Earthwalk have noticed the trend and are beginning to publish all of their maps with finer longitude and latitude graduations to aid in GPS navigation. Trails Illustrated has gone one step further by publishing selected waypoint coordinates on their maps, such as the specific coordinates for each of the 10th Mountain Ski Huts in Colorado.

By publishing specific coordinates, this will allow anyone to hone in on a potentially difficult-to-find location quickly and efficiently. Locations such as trailheads, emergency facilities, and side canyons. will be included on many of the newer maps published by private mapmakers.

The implications of GPS have not been lost on the entire publishing world either, and I don't imagine that the time is too far off when guidebooks will begin using specific latitude and longitude or UTM coordinates to help readers find trailheads and specific points using a GPS system. After all, marine charts and books have been doing it for years; why not wilderness ones?

With GPS comes computerization, or certainly the consideration of it. Currently, a number of companies around the country are testing computerized maps in cars—computerized maps that utilize a GPS system to plot a vehicle's progress on the road and help a driver to find specific destinations. The possibilities of other applications beyond urban navigation are limitless.

There are those who believe that the future will allow electronic maps to be purchased on-line and downloaded onto a personal computer. However, until compression and transmission technology improve, gaining access to maps via modem technology remains but a dream.

DeLorme, the publisher of the famous DeLorme Atlas & Gazetteers for each state has been into computer mapping technology for some time now. In fact, their StreetAtlas USA is a CD-ROM based street map of the entire country that can be instantly searched using zip code, place name, or even phone number. This map system is useful to the wilderness traveler as it gives remote road access to various parks and wilderness regions around the country. Find the general area you need, zoom in on it, select the correct location, and then print the page—it's that simple.

Still, GPS and computer navigation systems are somewhat cumbersome to use in a field application. Elegance in the system must be incorporated before anyone really accepts the combination of computerized mapping in conjunction with GPS. A number of companies, with the most recognized name of the bunch being DeLorme, have the most incredible GPS and intelligent navigation software that sells for around $500, but you must also have a laptop computer, a portable CD-ROM drive, and a portable GPS that will integrate with the system—and that is a mess of boxes and wires and cables to be lugging around in your car.

There are few who will argue, though, that once someone creates a portable system that is all-inclusive and contained in an easy-to-carry box, the logic and attraction of using such a system from the car to the trail will be too hard to resist.

It doesn't take a genius to begin to imagine the possibilities beyond GPS. How about a deluxe navigational system no bigger than a stopwatch? Combine an electronic compass with an altimeter and possibly some type of pedometer that would allow for dead reckoning calculations, and you will have quite a tool. Dream a little more. If you link that same electronic compass to a GPS and program it to save all the strikes and dips throughout the day and calculate bearings taking into account declination adjustments, and if this same compass will beep when you walk off the set bearing, you begin to have the makings of a near ideal wilderness navigational system.

How many years down the road is such an electronic compass system? Not too far. As we speak, I have seen prototypes that indicate a first model or two is just around the corner. At what price? Like the GPS, they are likely to begin on the pricey side—$150 to $200 dollars for a base model—and like the GPS, they are likely to spiral down in cost as the years tick by.

Appendix

- **Resource Listing**
  Electronic Compasses
  Hand-held GPS Systems
  Hand-held Compasses
  Maps
- **Metric Conversions**
- **Commonly Used Map Scales**
- **Azimuth Rings**
- **Magnetic World Variation Chart**
- **Map Series Comparison**
- **Topographical Maps Printed Since 1992**

RESOURCE LISTING

Electronic Compasses

Nexus: 307/856-6559
Precise Navigation: 415/903-1499

Hand-held GPS Systems

Brunton: 307/856-6559
Magellan: 909/394-5000
Trimble: 800/827-8000
Garmin: 913/599-1617
Sony: 800/342-5721
Eagle/Lowrance: 800/324-1354

Hand-held Compasses

Brunton: 307/856-6559
Silva: 607/779-2264
Sun: 800/441-0132
Suunto: 619/931-6788
Nexus: 307/856-6559

Maps

- United States Geological Survey (USGS) - 800/USA-Maps.
  Topographic maps covering almost all of the United States.
- United States Forest Service, Public Affairs Office -
  202/205-1760. Maps of all the national forests.
- National Park Service (NPS) - 202/208-4747.
  Maps of all the national parks.
- Bureau of Land Management, Public Affairs Office -
  202/343-5717. Maps of all the BLM lands.
- Canada Map Office - 613/952-7000. Topographic maps for all
  of Canada and the Northwest Territories.
- Map Link - 805/965-4402. One of the best sources of obscure
  maps for anywhere in the world. If you are heading somewhere
  and can't find a map, even if it is in the United States, give
  Map Link a call. Chances are, if a map is in print, they can
  locate it for you—for a price of course.

- Trails Illustrated - 800/962-1643. Waterproof and, in my opinion, the most up-to-date topographic maps of our nation's national parks as well as many recreation and wilderness areas.
- Tom Harrison Cartography - 415/456-7940. Excellent topographic maps of parks and wilderness areas in California.
- Earthwalk Press - 701/442-0503. Topographic maps for Western parks and wilderness areas as well as recreational areas in Hawaii.
- Appalachian Trail Conference - 304/535-6331. Topographic maps of the Appalachian Trail as it winds its way through the fourteen states.
- Wilderness Press - 510/843-8080. Topographic maps that coincide with their excellent field guides for the Sierra and other areas in California.
- DeLorme Mapping - 207/865-4171. Topographic atlases for most of the fifty states. Excellent resource for planning purposes.
- Wildflower Productions - 415/282-9112. CD-ROM maps for Yosemite, the San Francisco area, and others. Excellent!

METRIC CONVERSIONS

1 millimeter (mm) = .039 inch
1 inch = 254 millimeters (mm)
1 centimeter (cm) = .394 inch
1 inch = 2.54 centimeters (cm)
1 meter (m) = 39.37 inches / 3.28 feet / 1.09 yards
1 foot = .305 meter (m)
1 yard = .914 meter (m)
1 kilometer (km) = 3,281 feet / .62 mile
1 mile = 1.61 kilometer (km)

COMMONLY USED MAP SCALES

1:15,000 meters scale (most often for Orienteering)
1:24,000 scale; 7.5 minute USGS map
1:25,000 meters scale
1:50,000 meters scale
1:62,500 scale; 15 minute USGS map
1:63,600 meters scale
(See Appendix Figure A–3)

AZIMUTH RINGS

0–360 degrees - Global/Universal
Quads (4 x 0–90 degrees - Geological/Surveying
Mils (0–64^{00}) – Military = 1 yard at 1,000 yards
   or 17.777 miles = 1°
Grads (0–400 grads) = European

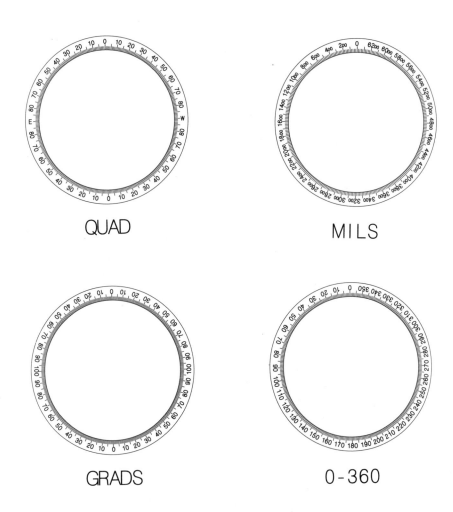

QUAD   MILS

GRADS   0-360

Figure A–1

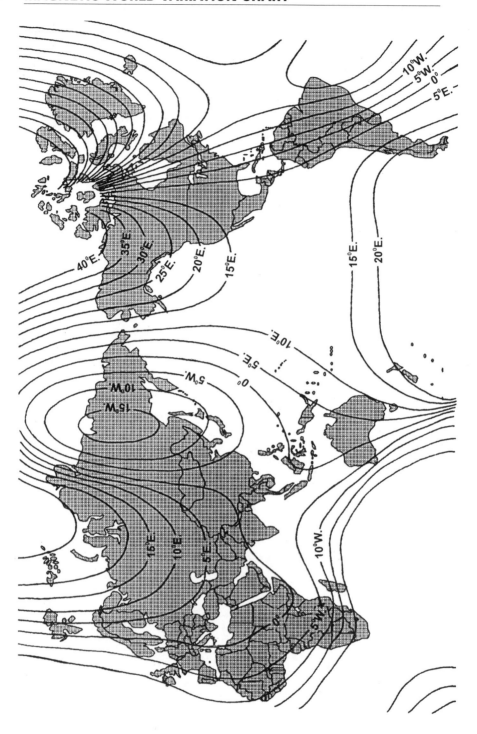

Figure A–2

MAP SERIES COMPARISON

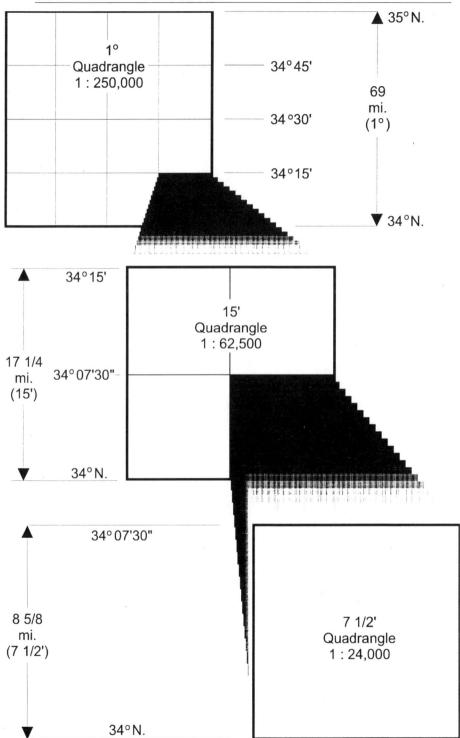

Figure A–3

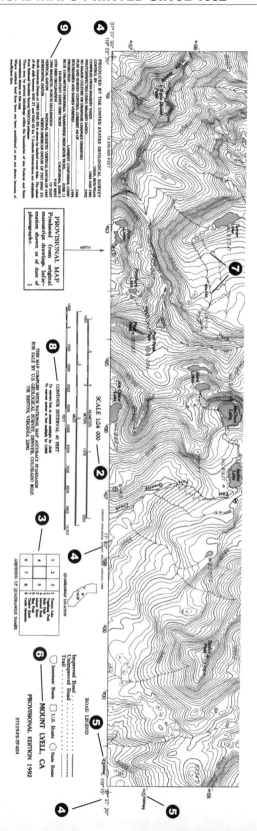

Figure A–4

 # Glossary of Terms

GLOSSARY OF TERMS

Altimeter: An instrument that measures elevation by using barometric (air) pressure.

Azimuth: Same as bearing. Refers to the degree of bearing from your current position to a landmark or destination. Reversing the bearing would be known as a back azimuth or back bearing.

Azimuth Ring: See Housing.

Back bearing: The 180-degree opposite of the azimuth or bearing. Also known as back azimuth.

Back sighting: What you do when you are establishing a back bearing.

Baseplate: The see-through plate of an orienteering compass onto which the compass housing is mounted.

Bearing: The direction of travel from your current position to a landmark or destination expressed in degrees from 1 to 360. Same as azimuth.

Bench mark: A permanent (as permanent as things can be in this world) object that is either natural or man-made and has a known elevation that can be used as a reference point when navigating.

Boxing the needle: A term that refers to placing the red end of the magnetic needle exactly over the red end of the orienting arrow when determining a bearing. Since the orienting arrow is slightly larger than the magnetic needle, we refer to having "boxed" the magnetic needle in. Some books or manuals will refer to this as "red on red" or "centering" the needle.

Cardinal points: The four main points of direction on a compass are North, 360 degrees; East, 90 degrees; South, 180 degrees; and West, 270 degrees.

Clinometer: A feature found on some compasses that allows the compass to measure vertical angles (such as the slope of a hill). Clinometers can also be used as a level.

Contour interval: The difference in elevation (height) between one contour line and the next. This interval is either expressed in feet or meters.

Contour line: Each contour line comprises an often irregular closed loop that connects points of equal elevation. The line with a darker shade of brown, typically every fifth line, is called an index contour and usually has the elevation printed on it. Elevations refer to elevation above sea level.

Declination: The difference in degrees between magnetic north (the direction the magnetic needle on a compass points) and true or geographic north (the direction maps are printed towards).

Depression: A natural or man-made hole in the ground which may or may not have a wet bottom. Depressions are shown on topographic maps by a contour line with small hachure marks pointing inward.

Direction-of-travel arrow: The arrow engraved or painted onto the front of the baseplate of the compass that is designed to indicate the direction you should hike when a bearing has been established or the direction you should point the compass to establish a bearing.

Hachure: Short lines used to represent relief features that lie in the direction of the steepest slope.

Housing: The rotating part of the compass that holds the damping fluid and the magnetic needle and has degrees engraved around its edge from 1 to 360. Also known as the Azimuth Ring.

Index line: The point at which the direction-of-travel arrow meets the housing and where the degree reading should be read to establish a bearing.

Latitude: The distance in degrees north and south from the equator. These lines run laterally (horizontally) around the globe and parallel the equator. One minute of latitude equals one nautical mile.

Longitude: The distance in degrees east and west from the prime meridian established in Greenwich, England. These lines run vertically (lengthwise) around the globe and connect each pole.

Magnetic lines: Lines drawn onto a topographic map by the user to indicate the direction of magnetic north and to allow the map to speak the same directional language as the compass.

Magnetic north: The geographical region towards which all magnetic needles point. This point is approximately thirteen hundred miles south of true north and moves slightly each year due to the earth's rotation and the friction created between its solid crust and liquid center.

Map projection: The process of transforming a round object (the earth) into a flat object (a map) with the least amount of distortion. There is always some distortion caused in this process which is why grid lines are not perfectly parallel.

Meridian: An imaginary line circling the earth and passing through the geographic poles. All points on any meridian will have the same longitude.

Orienteering: Using a map and compass in the field to determine your route of travel. Has commonly come to mean a type of competition at which competitors try to navigate across challenging terrain from point to point arriving at the finish first.

Orienting a map: Turning the map so that it represents a one-dimensional image that comes as close as possible to exactly paralleling the three-dimensional world you are standing in.

Orienting arrow: The north/south pointing arrow engraved or painted in red or black into the housing. It is slightly wider than the magnetic needle and is used to "box" or surround the magnetic needle when establishing a bearing.

Orienting lines: The lines on the bottom of the compass housing that parallel the orienting arrow.

Parallel of latitude: An imaginary line that circles the earth parallel to the equator. All points on a given parallel have the same latitude.

Position fix: Sometimes referred to as fixing your position. This means establishing your exact position on a map in terms of a coordinate system such as latitude / longitude or UTM.

Prime meridian: This is the meridian that runs through Greenwich, England, at a longitude of zero degrees and is used as the position of origin for measurements of longitude.

Prismatic compass: A compass with a mirror designed to allow a user to see both distant objects being sighted and the compass face at the same time.

Protractor: Sometimes built into a compass, this instrument allows you to determine and measure angles in degrees and is most useful when projecting magnetic lines across your map.

Quadrangle: A four-sided section of land bounded by parallels of latitude and meridians of longitude depicted on or by a topographic map. Topo maps are sometimes referred to as "quads."

Relief: Changes in terrain.

Relief shading: A process of shading the map so that it takes on a three-dimensional look. Typically, maps are shaded as if the light source casting the shadow is coming from the northwest.

Scale: The distance between two points on a map as they relate to the distance between those two points on the earth.

Sighting line: Sometimes called the line of sight, this refers to the imaginary line that you sight along to take your bearing.

True North: Also known as geographic north—the North Pole.

Waypoint: A checkpoint used as a point of reference for GPS.

Notes

Notes

Notes

Notes

Notes

Notes